GUIDELINES

GEOGRAPHY INTO PRACTICE

ELISABETH HACKING

Acknowledgements

I would like to acknowledge the important contributions of Graham Corney, Eleanor Rawlings and GSIP teachers to my thinking about the National Curriculum for geography and, in particular, Louise Robinson for her collaboration in the preparation for Chapter 3 and the example course outline (Figure 2). I would also like to thank Andy Owen for contributing his unit of work on wind energy (Chapter 5) and its assessment (Chapter 6). Finally, I acknowledge the support of many other friends and colleagues including Julie Turner and Jeanette Wade.

ISBN 0582 08826 7
First published 1992
Second impression 1993
© Longman Group UK Limited 1992

Set in 11/12 point Plantin
Typeset by Typewise Photosetting, York
Printed in Malaysia by TCP

Contents

1 Geography into Practice: Introduction

There has been much controversy surrounding the National Curriculum for geography since its early days as a consultation document developed by the geography Working Group (DES, June 1990). It was finally published in the form of a statutory Order in March 1991 (DES). Since September 1991 teachers have been expected to implement the geography Order for pupils in Year 7 (Y7) (the first year of key stage 3). By 1995 all the year groups in key stage 3 (KS3) and KS4 will be following the National Curriculum for geography.

Many teachers have been critical of the content of this 'new' curriculum and have not welcomed this major initiative to an already overburdened profession. Nevertheless, it has provoked some useful thinking and engendered debate on the nature and purpose of geography. It has also provided teachers with an opportunity to review their current practice and consider the direction of geography education in their school.

The author's view is that the way forward is to look for the opportunities in and make the most of the geography Order. Therefore, this book aims to help secondary geography teachers make sense of and develop the National Curriculum for geography, working from their own philosophy of the subject and building on their existing curriculum and expertise. It is written with a number of people in mind, including beginning teachers, classroom teachers, heads of department/faculties and those involved in setting up INSET activities.

This book is divided into five further chapters, each of which is designed to address issues that are currently being debated by geography teachers. Chapter 2 attempts to review different views of geography and the developments in school geography during the last twenty-five years. This should provoke thought about teachers' own views of the subject and how they might put this into practice when developing the National Curriculum for geography. In addition, it will help put the National Curriculum itself into perspective. Chapter 3 is about becoming familiar with the geography Order and reviewing the existing curriculum. The next chapters consider successive levels of planning with practical ideas for implementing the geography Order: Chapter 4 includes key stage course outlines, Chapter 5 units of work, and Chapter 6 lesson ideas. Although there is a logical sequence, there is no reason why teachers cannot use chapters and sections individually as the need arises.

At the end of each chapter are tasks and questions relating to the theme of the chapter. These can be used in a number of ways. Ideally they are designed to be used as INSET activities, either in departmental meetings, on non-contact days or with other groups of teachers (e.g. beginning teachers, cluster groups, LEA training days). Alternatively, they can be dipped into by any individual teacher who is attempting to plan and implement the geography Order.

When using the book it would be helpful to have the following documents at hand:

- NCC (1991) *Geography Non-statutory Guidance.* NCC;

- DES (1991a) *Geography for ages 5 to 16.* HMSO (the statutory Order);

- DES (1991b) *Geography in the National Curriculum: A short course for pupils at KS4.* (HMSO).

It is further suggested that teachers use the information supplied by the Geographical Association (e.g. in *Teaching Geography)* when planning and implementing the National Curriculum for geography.

The purpose of this chapter is to attempt to define geography and determine the contribution it makes to the education of the 11–16 age range. The developments in school geography in the last twenty-five years will also be reviewed to provide a perspective to the introduction of the National Curriculum for geography.

The nature and purpose of geography

A definition of geography

The newspaper article extract in Figure 1 illustrates how different people view geography in different ways. The populist view is that geography involves the learning of facts and figures about different places. However, a subject is more than facts. Any subject has a field of enquiry, a set of concepts and ideas, and ways of thinking and working.

Experts are worlds apart on geography

By Sue Surkes
Education Correspondent

MORE mature readers will know that Monrovia is the capital of Liberia. Younger ones may not.

This has nothing to do with intelligence, but with the way children were, and are, taught geography.

Twenty years ago, the study of Africa would have meant identifying the Orange Free State, the Zambezi River, Mount Kilimanjaro and the Gold and Ivory coasts.

Nowadays, it is more concerned with debating great issues – famine, poverty and how to save the planet.

Figure 1: *Extract from* The Sunday Correspondent, *4 February 1990*

Most geography teachers would agree that geography is about people and the environment. It includes the study of physical and human processes that shape the environment, places and patterns at the earth's surface, and the people who live there. For some teachers the study of the interactions between physical and human characteristics is at the heart of the subject. These teachers believe that geographers should study physical and human interactions within the environment and the issues, questions or problems arising from them (see examples in Figure 1). This is because peoples' use of the environment often creates change and conflict, so investigations would not be complete without recognition of resulting issues.

To summarise, although geography overlaps other subject areas geographers do think and work in specific ways. Firstly, they approach the study of people and the environment in specific ways and ask specific questions. Secondly, they are particularly interested in patterns of location and distinctiveness of places. Thirdly, they take a bridging role between subjects which study either physical or human characteristics.

The purpose of geographical education

Elements of learning

Geography contributes different elements of learning to a young person's education, including:

- knowledge and understanding;
- skills;
- values and attitudes.

Knowledge and understanding

If geography is about people and environment topics and issues then it must have a huge amount to offer young people who are trying to make sense of their world. Every day the media bombards us with information and crises from home and further afield which relate to people and the environment. Geography helps young people understand the causes and importance of these issues in the news. However, geography does not just help with understanding the news. HMI claims that:

> *Geography helps pupils to make sense of their surroundings and to gain a better appreciation and understanding of the variety of physical and human conditions on the earth's surface.*

DES,1986, p.1

Values

Many teachers emphasise the importance of values education arising from the study of geography. They argue that helping pupils to develop and clarify their attitudes and values towards people, places, the environment and related issues is crucial. In doing so, pupils are prepared for life as responsible and tolerant citizens within a multicultural society. Further, it empowers them to take actions which could make the world a better place.

Skills

Through the investigation of people–environment topics and issues in geography lessons, young people are able to develop and practice a range of skills including practical, intellectual and social skills in addition to those associated with literacy, numeracy and graphicacy.

- *Practical skills* are often used when pupils are engaged in observation tasks, perhaps using equipment such as clinometers during fieldwork.

- *Intellectual skills* are used when pupils are enquiring into issues, questions or problems by developing their own questions or hypotheses; considering data needed; describing and analysing data; evaluating findings; making decisions or drawing conclusions.

- *Social skills* are developed through ways of working together such as co-operative groups and interactions with people from the community.

- *Literacy and numeracy skills* are practised whenever pupils are communicating or processing information.

- *Graphicacy skills* are of particular value since they allow communication of spatial information that cannot be conveyed as well, verbally or numerically. Although graphicacy is developed in other areas of the curriculum (e.g. craft, design and technology), geography does have a particular contribution as mapping is an integral part of geography teaching and learning. More detailed discussion of graphicacy can be found in the writings of Balchin (1972) and Boardman (1983).

Changes in school geography: the last twenty-five years

As implied in the newspaper article in Figure 1, school geography has moved from rote learning of facts about places to investigating people–environment issues and questions. This section attempts to briefly document these changes and to discover what caused them.

Academic geography

Geography has moved through a number of traditions in the last twenty-five years so many new ideas and techniques have been diffused into the classroom.

The areal tradition

Prior to 1965 the 'areal tradition' was dominant. This was associated with the study of different areas and regions of the world. Influential in the development of this tradition was A. J. Herbertson and his 'natural regions' (1905).

In schools this tradition was often associated with an approach to teaching and learning in which pupils were recipients of information from the teacher. Lesson content included the physical characteristics of each region studied and how people responded to them. Textbooks associated with this approach include Dudley Stamp's *Regional Geography* courses (1930–63).

The spatial tradition

In the 1960s a new tradition took over, known as the 'spatial tradition'. This change in the dominant tradition is often referred to as the 'quantitative revolution'. It was a reaction against the descriptive nature of 'regional geography' and a move towards attempting to find patterns in space using quantitative techniques. In this way the geographer could build models to simplify reality and explain patterns and processes. The academic geographers Richard Chorley and Peter Haggett did much to encourage teachers to take on these 'new' ideas (see Chorley's *Frontiers in Geography Teaching*, 1965).

When this tradition got through to classrooms it resulted in a changed teaching and learning approach with pupils involved in manipulating data and using techniques in order to develop, prove, or disprove theories. Teachers spent less time transmitting information and more time assisting pupils and explaining different techniques. Textbooks using these 'new' techniques include Bradford and Kent's *Human Geography* (1977).

The people–environment tradition

The 1970s and early 1980s saw a reaction on the part of some geographers against the spatial tradition, since it was seen to depersonalise the subject. There was a move towards a 'humanistic' approach in which the feelings, perceptions and values of individual people were seen to be essential for understanding the changing environment. The work of Yi Fu Tuan, for example, is associated with this approach (1974). This saw a move away from studying people and their environment separately and towards studying people–environment topics or issues.

At the same time those who traditionally saw themselves as 'physical geographers' were showing a greater interest in applied geography. In this, understanding issues and solving problems of current concern was becoming more important than simply understanding physical processes. One example of applied geography is the investigations of natural hazards conducted by White (1974). White and other applied physical geographers were also bridging the gap between the study of people (human geography) and the study of the environment (physical geography).

More recently, the 'ecological' approach has become popular. This involves the use of systems theory to describe and explain the workings of environments and the interrelationship of living and non-living elements within them. In this way management strategies for environments at different scales can be developed. For an example of this approach, see Simmons' *The Ecology of Natural Resources* (1974).

The people–environment tradition resulted in an approach to teaching and learning in which pupils investigate people–environment issues and topics using a variety of techniques (e.g. values enquiry, quantitative techniques, systems theory). Furthermore, they are encouraged to think about other peoples' reactions and feelings towards places and issues as well as their own. A good example of a textbook using this approach is *Worldwide Issues in Geography,* edited by Clive Hart (1985).

The 'critical' tradition

In the last ten to fifteen years some academic geographers have taken up 'welfare' and 'radical' approaches. Their investigations focus on social inequalities (e.g. in access to resources or services, differences in quality of life, wealth distribution). Welfare geographers describe findings of social inequality and attempt to explain the causes of them (see Coates *et al.*, 1977). 'Radical' geographers use Marxism to interpret issues of social inequality. Furthermore, they suggest action to reduce inequalities, rather than simply explaining the reasons for them (see Peet, 1977).

These recent developments in academic Geography have again influenced teaching and learning approaches in some classrooms. Here, pupils are given the opportunity to think 'critically'. This involves pupils enquiring into people–environment issues and the resulting inequalities. In order to do this pupils are encouraged not to accept anything at face value; to ask critical questions; make decisions; and suggest or take action in relation to their findings and conclusions. Probably the best textbook example of the 'critical' approach is the *Geography Today* series (Clammer *et al.*, 1991).

Teaching and learning

The last twenty-five years have also seen important changes in teaching and learning strategies as a result of new ideas about learning theory and the needs of individuals. The work of influential psychologists (e.g. Bruner, 1966, and Piaget and Inhelder, 1969) made educationalists think both about the process of learning and the development of the child. For example, ideas about how children develop from concrete to abstract thinkers resulted in geography teachers reassessing how early they could introduce different types of maps. Ideas about the process of learning resulted in teachers developing ways of sequencing learning like the enquiry approach (see pp.30–32).

Other influential thinking included that of Douglas Barnes and others, summarised in the Bullock Report (1975). In this, a case for pupils making sense of their learning through talk was strongly argued and justified. In classrooms there was a resulting trend to encourage pupils to talk with peers through group work.

Wider issues, such as the underachievement of working class pupils, girls and black pupils also raised concerns of how to make education more accessible for all. For example, the Rampton Report (1981) found pupils of West Indian origin to be significantly underachieving. These concerns led to strategies for 'multicultural' education, in particular anti-racist and anti-sexist approaches in which racism and sexism are tackled head on. Examples of these approaches can be found in various volumes of *Contemporary Issues in Geography and Education* (e.g. Gill, 1983) and also in Hacking (1991).

These changing ideas about teaching and learning added fuel to the development in school geography away from a 'descriptive' curriculum and towards a 'critical' curriculum.

Curriculum development projects

At the same time the quantitative revolution got underway in schools, the Schools Council of Curriculum and Examinations funded a number of geography projects. In 1970 two Geography projects were launched:

- Geography for the Young School Leaver (GYSL) was set up to look at the contribution of the subject to pupils of average and below average ability at a time when the school-leaving age was being raised. The project team started from the needs of young people, then looked for relevant contributions from the discipline (see Beddis and Dalton, 1974).

- The Geography 14–18 Project (Bristol Project) was aimed initially at more able pupils. This project team looked for ways to incorporate new geography into the classroom (see Hickman *et al.*, 1977).

In both cases the projects promoted active, enquiry learning. This was encouraged through the investigation of a range of social, political and environmental issues leading to the development of knowledge and understanding, skills, and attitudes and values.

These, along with other influential projects such as the Schools Council 16 to 19 Project, the Geography Schools and Industry Project (GSIP) and Development Education projects, gave more autonomy to the teacher to take a central role in the process of curriculum development.

In addition to these geography projects, curriculum development with a strong integrated humanities ethos was also going on. An example of this was the Humanities Curriculum Project. One of the main emphases in this was the child-centred approach to teaching and learning (see Stenhouse, 1970).

Though these developments had a very positive impact on school geography some teachers would say that they did not go far enough in empowering pupils to take control of their own learning and become informed and active citizens with at least some control of their future.

Other influences

Although academic geography and educational concerns have had a powerful impact on school geography there have been underlying influences as a result of a rapidly changing world. The 'green movement' and global concern over the increasing inequality of life between and within different countries and places have again promoted a more critical geography in which controversial issues are investigated and solutions or action suggested by pupils (see the Global Environmental Education Programme co-ordinated for the World Wide Fund (WWF) by John Huckle, 1988. See also *Global Teacher, Global Learner* by Graham Pike and David Selby (1988). At the same time, increasing wealth and leisure opportunities for some has encouraged leisure and recreation to be incorporated into school geography.

Changing technology and pressure for vocational training has led to money becoming available for technological and vocational developments (e.g. links with industry) at a time of scarce resources. The use of information technology (IT) allows for rapid accessibility and manipulation of large amounts of data so improving the information available to pupils.

Conclusion

Recently, John Huckle provided 'eight reasons to be cheerful' about the progress made in geographical education in the last ten years (1991). He also suggested work still to be done. Some of this is summarised below.

Progress in geographical education and some further goals

1 Multicultural, anti-racist and anti-sexist elements have been introduced. Issues of class also need introducing, for example the reshaping of class differences 'and their geographical expression' as a result of government policy.

2 The growth of a 'critical' curriculum and introduction of some progressive textbooks (e.g. Clammer's *Geography Today*, 1987). More widespread development of 'a social education which facilitates critical and active citizenship' is still needed.

3 Curriculum development which 'encouraged teachers and pupils to reflect and act on a troubled world' (see Fisher, *World Studies* 8–13 (1983) and develop a critical political and economic awareness (see Corney and GSIP teachers, 1991).

4 The realisation of the need for 'ecologically sustainable development'. Further work is needed to introduce to pupils why this is needed and how it can be achieved.

Clearly, this is a personal view, but it provides a useful review of progress in school geography in the last ten years and suggests further developments that should be implemented if pupils are to be empowered to contribute to and improve society.

Now for the first time, the Government is overtly influencing what happens in geography classrooms with the introduction of the National Curriculum. Neverthless, there is scope for working from the philosophy and approach of individual teachers and building on the positive developments experienced in school geography during the last twenty-five years. Methods of doing this will be suggested in the following chapters.

Q **Tasks**

Refer to the section on changes in school geography in the last twenty-five years and consider your departmental aims and your own view of geography education.

1 Which of the traditions or approaches described in the section most reflects your own/your department's philosophy?

2 Do you think this is the most appropriate approach for 11 to 16 year olds? Why?

3 Which direction would you like to move in and why? (you might like to develop your departmental aims further). Refer to the statutory Order for geography p. iii (attainment target headings) and read pp.41–46 (programme of study for KS3).

4 Decide which tradition(s) of geography seem most apparent in the Order. Discuss the implications of this.

3 The National Curriculum for geography: what now?

This chapter aims to:

- introduce the structure and terminology of the National Curriculum for geography;
- help teachers become more familiar with its entitlement for the 11 to 16 age range;
- suggest a method for reviewing the existing 11 to 16 curriculum;
- help identify elements which need strengthening or introducing into the curriculum.

Also, consideration will be made of how it fits into the wider curriculum and possible priorities suggested for becoming familiar with other documents.

Structure and terminology

The geography folder should contain both the *Non-statutory Guidance* and the statutory Order. The *Non-statutory Guidance* is intended to help teachers implement the Order. The Order itself includes both attainment targets (ATs) and programmes of study for each key stage.

Attainment targets

Each of the attainment targets represents a particular component of geography which pupils need to learn about and will be assessed on. There are five geography attainment targets:

- Geographical Skills;
- Knowledge and Understanding of Places;
- Physical;
- Human;
- Environmental Geography.

Therefore, there are three types of attainment target relating to different components of geography: skills, places and themes. Physical, human and environmental geography represent the theme attainment targets. In the last chapter it was suggested that the various traditions of geography and their associated approaches to teaching and learning are all still to be found in school geography. It is interesting to note the influence of these traditions on the attainment targets. For example, the place attainment target would seem to link to the 'areal' tradition and the environmental one to the 'people–environment' tradition.

Statements of attainment

Within each attainment target there are statements of attainment, against which pupils will be assessed. These are pitched at ten levels of attainment and represent a ladder of progression for each key stage. For KS3 (ages 11–14) pupils should be working between levels 3 and 7, and for KS4 (ages 14–16), levels 4 and 10. Clearly some pupils will fall outside these ranges and can be awarded success at any level, though the teaching package should be directed towards the specified levels.

Programmes of study

There is a programme of study for each key stage set out with the requirements of each of the components of geography (places, themes and skills). In addition, maps of Britain, Europe and the world show what locations pupils should be able to identify at each key stage. Together this represents the content of the teaching programme for that age range. The programmes of study for KS3 and KS4 relate directly to the specified levels (3–7 and 4–10 respectively) and so there is overlap in the requirements of the two key stages. Since the range of ability will be wide in any year group, extension work is specified for the highest levels (see the statutory Order, p.41, no.4, for an example of this from the Geographical Skills section of the programme of study for KS3).

Teaching and learning strategies

There is little specification in the programme of study about the teaching and learning strategies to be used. Teachers therefore have scope to use preferred strategies.

Teaching and learning about place

As mentioned in Chapter 2, the areal tradition and associated teaching approaches have mostly disappeared from school geography. Therefore, for many teachers the idea of teaching about places and locations for their own sake will be a new one. Reviewing and evaluating how pupils in their classes currently develop a knowledge of places and locations could be especially helpful. Developing this knowledge through the study of themes is one way of going about it.

Enquiry teaching and learning

One teaching and learning strategy that is specified in the programme of study is enquiry. For KS3 it states that 'an enquiry approach should be adopted for classroom activities ...' (DES, 1991a, p. 41 no.1) and pupil-led enquiries are a feature of KS4.

The sequence below illustrates how the Working Group saw enquiry. This implies a process for learning, though they stressed that it is not a rigid sequence – it can be used in part, and can be a small-scale project or last for many weeks.

Some important elements of enquiry

- recognising an issue or focus for enquiry;
- formulating appropriate questions – giving the enquiry direction;
- collecting relevant information;
- interpreting and analysing information;
- drawing conclusions, offering explanations and, if appropriate, proposing actions;
- presenting findings and conclusions;
- evaluating the enquiry;
- considering the implications of findings and conclusions for personal assumptions, understandings, attitudes and values.

DES 1990, p.47

Organising the content

Again, there is little direction about how to organise the content of the teaching programme. Teachers normally do this by dividing programmes into topics or issues. However, it seems clear from a variety of documents that the three components of geography – skills, places and themes – should be combined. It is also suggested that either themes or places take the lead and skills are simply incorporated into this (DES, 1990, p.47). The method of organising the content will therefore depend on a teacher's preferred approaches to geography, as reviewed in Chapter 2.

The three main approaches possible are:

> 1 'regional' with units of work organised by place;
>
> 2 'thematic' organised around human, physical or 'environmental' geography themes;
>
> 3 'issue-based' including issues, questions or problems which emphasise (yet combine) different components of geography.

In the case of the regional approach it would be necessary to incorporate themes, and for the thematic approach, places. With an issue-based approach the emphasis may vary, though in most cases an issue would involve both a place and a theme. However, issues are not exclusive to the third approach. It would be possible to incorporate issues into either of the other two approaches. Some teachers may decide to opt for a combination of approaches, as suggested in the *Non-statutory Guidance* (NCC, 1991, p.C8).

Becoming familiar with specific requirements for each key stage

During the familiarisation process the best place to start is the programmes of study. There is little point in going straight to what will be assessed (attainment targets and statements of attainment); it is much better to start with what has to be in the teaching programme. Resource 1 provides a summary of the main emphases in the programmes of study for KS3 and should help give an idea of the entitlement for this age group.

It is important not to lose sight of valuable developments in school geography and teachers should consider what they appreciate most at present in terms of:

- teaching and learning strategies;
- particular units of work;
- resources;
- teacher expertise in the department;
- fieldwork;
- use of the local area and community.

This review can be used to look for the opportunities to continue to develop the most valued aspects. It is important to check what is done now against the programme of study emphases in order to identify what can be used again (e.g. topics, resources or approaches to teaching and learning), what needs adapting, and what needs introducing (see Tasks on p.15).

Geography element	Emphasis	Relationship with existing curriculum		
		already included	partly included	not included
Skills	■ Enquiry approach using primary and secondary sources			
	■ Use of IT			
	■ Observing, recording and measuring: weather small-scale features			
	■ Selecting information and describing patterns and relationships from: maps and diagrams (including atlases/OS 1:50,000 1:25,000) aerial photographs statistics *satellite images*			
	■ Drawing/constructing: cross sections fieldsketches simple sketch maps *annotated sketch maps*			
Places	Scale: regional and country with some smaller case studies ■ Home region: overview, economic activities, development and change (and local area enquiries) *decision making and change*			
	■ EC (France, Germany, Italy or Spain): overview of one country: compare two regions, study one locality *(theme study: agriculture, regional development, tourism)*			
	■ EDC: overview of one country (see geography Order, p.43 no.12) and study changes in one locality; *issues of development*			
	■ USA/USSR/Japan: comparative overview for one: manufacturing and energy *environmental problems arising from industry*			
	■ *International trade: main patterns*			
Physical	■ landforms and processes plate techtonics rivers *or* coasts sediment movement/weathering and erosion			
	■ hydrology watercycling flooding and human response			
	■ climate and weather UK and three other types *anticyclone, depression*			
	■ biogeography soils *and erosion* three vegetation types			
	■ one hazard cause, consequence, response			
Human	■ population global patterns migration *recent large-scale* change (region, country)			
	■ transport compare different types routes/networks *consequence of change*			
	■ settlement location/patterns/functions/hierarchy change urban land use – issues of change *and impact on people*			
	■ economic activity shops (location and land use) farms manufacturing – employment structure and change – land use conflict issue – development levels			
Environmental	■ natural resoures impact of use on environment (especially two energy sources) water quality/quantity *impact of technology*			
	■ management strategies e.g. valuable environments pollution *leisure impact*			
	■ *global issues of environmental change*			

Resource 1: *Emphases in the KS3 programme of study (italics denotes work towards level 7)*

A note about key stage 4

The requirements for KS4 are less straightforward since pupils in this age range can select a number of options incuding:

- a full course in either history or geography leading to a GCSE or equivalent qualification;
- short courses in history and geography, not necessarily combined together (e.g. geography could be combined with a short course in technology) leading to a joint/modular GCSE or other SEAC certification.

This means that students who select to study a full course in history need not study any geography. Schools, however, must offer both history and geography at KS4.

The supplementary Orders for the short course in geography have been sent to schools and should be added to the geography ringbinder (DES, 1991b). This is a shortened version of the original KS4 Orders including:

- a reduced number of statements of attainment from ATs 1, 2 and 5 (compulsory);
- a choice for teachers of strands from ATs 3 and 4 and their associated statements of attainment.

It is expected that examination boards will be rewriting GCSE syllabuses to take account of KS4 Orders. It is likely they will offer a combined GCSE in history and geography to enable students taking short courses in these subjects to attain a GCSE.

(For further information about implementing KS4 geography see advice from the Geography Association circulated with *Teaching Geography*, April 1992.)

The wider curriculum

The National Curriculum is made up of core and foundation subjects, religious education and cross-curricular elements. The cross-curricular elements are intended to be developed mainly at whole-school level and include Dimensions, Skills and Themes.

Dimensions

- personal and social development;
- equal opportunities/education for life in a multicultural society;
- should be explicit in the whole curriculum policy;
- are the responsibility of all teachers.

Skills

- communication;
- numeracy;
- study;
- problem solving;
- personal and social;
- IT.

Themes

- economic and industrial understanding;
- careers education and guidance;
- health education;
- education for citizenship;
- environmental education.

Cross-curricular elements

Clearly the Dimensions and Skills will inform the thinking and planning of all teachers, for example how to provide equal opportunities and meet the needs of individual pupils, or how to promote communication skills. Themes may be developed in different ways: through subjects, in special blocks of time, and through a personal and social development programme. Nevertheless, the geography department needs to consider how it can contribute to the Themes and build this into planning (as suggested in later chapters). Geography has valuable contributions to make to them all, and the Themes can also offer teaching and learning opportunities not apparent in the geography Order (e.g. in the field of values education).

Core and foundation subjects

There are links and overlaps between geography and other subjects especially technology, science and history. Again it is important at this stage to have some knowledge of this in order to work together to reinforce pupils' learning, avoid repetition, or teach an integrated or combined programme. In many schools at KS3 humanities teaching is the norm. There are still opportunities for history and geography teachers to collaborate and integrate some units of work. At this stage it is probably more realistic to have conversations with 'experts', than to plough through lots of subject documents. The *Non-statutory Guidance* provides further information about the overlaps and some suggestions of how to collaborate (pp.C15–18).

Key stage 2

If the experience of a pupil moving between key stages is to be a positive one with a smooth transition in learning then there is an obvious need for liaison between teachers of successive key stages. This is particularly crucial when it involves a school transfer and for many readers this will be at the KS2 to KS3 boundary. Many teachers and LEAs will have started the process of creating links with those responsible for geography in the feeder schools. The purpose of this is to share plans and ideas for teaching programmes, in addition to agreeing at least some of the content and approaches of the two key stages.

Conclusion

Before any planning commences it is clearly important for teachers to have some familiarity with the National Curriculum, including KS3 and KS4 programmes of study; what has gone before (KS2); other subjects (particularly history, science and technology); and cross-curricular elements. In addition, it is helpful to review the existing geography curriculum against National Curriculum requirements in order to build on departmental strengths. At the same time constraints imposed by the National Curriculum may come to light and teachers will have to consider how best to deal with them.

If geography departments are to have a clear vision of how to achieve their aims, maintain their philosophy (as reviewed in the Tasks, p.8) and develop the existing curriculum, this familiarisation and review process is crucial.

Q Tasks

1 As a department, identify and make a note important aspects of your current 11–14 curriculum, particularly those you most value. Include:

  ▪ teaching and learning strategies;

  ▪ how you teach about place;

  ▪ units of work;

  ▪ resources;

  ▪ fieldwork;

  ▪ use of the local area and community.

You might also like to consider the teacher expertise you most value (e.g. someone with travel or VSO experience, or an expert on river fieldwork) that is currently utilised or that you would like to use.

2 Refer to Resource 1 which provides the emphases of the KS3 programme of study. It might also be useful to have your department's existing syllabus documents handy. For each of the emphases described, record in the appropriate box whether your existing curriculum:

  a) already covers this;

  b) covers it in another age range or in part;

  c) does not include this.

This may be in the form of a tick or cross, or a brief comment.

3 Any crosses present in the right hand box of Resource 1 represent your targets for planning. Note them down and consider the priorities for resources this suggests.

4 Look back at your answers to question 1. Check the aspects of your existing 11 to 14 curriculum which you value against the emphases in Resource 1. If any do not immediately seem to fit in consider how you might allow them to.

5 On-going tasks are in the form of links and conversations to be set up. This includes:

  ▪ experts on the cross-curricular themes of citizenship, economic and industrial understanding, and environmental education;

  ▪ teachers of other subjects, especially history, science, technology and mathematics;

  ▪ teachers responsible for geography in the feeder schools.

One way of going about this is to divide labour in the department and report back to a meeting.

4 Planning a key stage course outline

The purpose of this chapter is to help teachers develop a course outline suitable for their school context whilst meeting the requirements of the National Curriculum. A course outline is a summary of a key stage teaching programme. Any teaching programme is divided into units of work, each of which has a particular theme or emphasis; for example, 'migration issues', national parks', or 'the Amazon rainforest'. A course outline consists of the headings of the units of work, together with a brief description of their objectives and contents.

In this chapter a step-by-step approach to developing a course outline is suggested. Figure 2 provides an example course outline developed in this way. It represents a teaching programme which uses an issue-based approach.

Figure 3 summarises the suggested steps to be taken when planning a course outline and should be used in conjunction with the whole of this chapter. It is sensible to plan the KS3 course outline first in order to think about progression issues when planning KS4.

Step 1: A starting-point

It is suggested in Figure 3 that teachers review their aims for geographical education, preferred teaching and learning approaches, and become familiar with both the National Curriculum and the wider curriculum before starting outline planning. These have been discussed in Chapters 2 and 3 and teachers may have completed the relevant tasks at the end of each chapter.

In Chapter 3 three possible approaches for organising the teaching programme were suggested: the 'regional', 'thematic' and 'issue-based' approaches. Enquiry must be incorporated into the teaching and learning programme and it is possible to include enquiry in any of these. It could be argued, however, that an issue-based approach is more appropriate since it gives a clear purpose to the enquiry.

Teachers need to decide which of these approaches they wish to adopt or continue using. Alternatively, it may be that a combination of these approaches is used (see Chapter 3, p.11).

Step 2: Generating ideas for units of work

This stage in planning involves the generation of ideas for the headings of units of work. The nature of the unit headings will depend upon a teacher's chosen approach. They will relate to places (e.g. 'Brazil'), themes (e.g. 'rivers') or issues (e.g. 'the impact of new developments on the local community and environment').

The number of units needed will depend on how teachers intend to break up each year of the key stage. For example, if in KS3 two units per term are preferred this will mean six per year and so eighteen in total. Alternatively, it would be possible to have an even number of hours for each unit, rather than the uneven half-terms, in which case more and shorter units could be used. The method selected may well be imposed by the timetable if a modular system is used.

Y7

	1 Local transport issues	2 Conflict in a local ecosystem	3 Issues arising from energy use	4 Impact of manufacturing change	5 Planning issues in built environments	6 Living in hazardous environments
Title						
Possible issue	Looking at the way in which changes in transport patterns are affecting the community and environment	Investigating whether a local ecosystem should be protected and how it could be improved	How the use of two energy resources creates costs and benefits for people and the environment	Investigating the changes arising from the location of new manufacturing industries	How urban problems can be overcome by planning	Why people live in hazardous environments and how the hazard can be managed
Possible emphasis theme/skill	▪ different types of transport ▪ routes and networks ▪ home region overview/development and change ▪ maps (OS) ▪ air photographs	▪ influences of weather and other site factors on ecosystems ▪ soils/weather/vegetation ▪ environmental management ▪ observing and measuring ▪ IT	▪ resources and impact of use ▪ two energy sources ▪ pollution ▪ atlas/maps ▪ statistics	▪ economy of home region and EDC ▪ development and change ▪ land use conflicts ▪ location and distribution of industry ▪ development levels ▪ atlas/maps (OS) ▪ local area enquiry ▪ IT database	▪ settlement patterns/functions/hierarchy/ migration ▪ changes/problems ▪ urban land use patterns and conflicts ▪ shopping patterns ▪ planning/improving the environment ▪ maps (OS) ▪ statistics	▪ plate tectonics: volcanoes and earthquakes ▪ cause of one hazard ▪ consequences and management ▪ migration ▪ development levels ▪ diagrams/world maps ▪ secondary sources
Scale/place	home region/locality of the home/school	locality of the home/school	regional/national (UK and EDC)	local/regional (home and EDC)	local/regional (home and EC)	local/regional (USSR)/global
Fieldwork/PFC link	planner/parents (as transport users)	pressure groups; on site fieldwork		pressure groups; local site visit	planners	
XCT Other sub.	EIU Citizenship Environmental ed. / History Maths	Environmental ed. Citizenship / Science	EIU Environmental ed. / Technology	EIU Citizenship / History	Citizenship EIU / Environmental ed.	EIU / Science

Y8

	7 Conflicts arising from agricultural change	8 Pressure on large-scale ecosystems	9 Water management	10 Economic development issues	11 Inequalities in urban areas	12 Conflicts at the coastline
Title						
Possible issue	How changes in farming practice create environmental and social conflicts and how these can be resolved	Investigating the impact of social, technological and economic change on tropical rainforest and tundra	Issues arising from water resource development and management	How a changing economic base affects people and the environment	How variations in quality of life (within and between cities) can be reduced	Investigating the need for coastal management and its impact
Possible emphasis theme/skill	▪ factors affecting agricultural land use patterns ▪ changes and conflicts ▪ climate, weather and soils ▪ statistics ▪ secondary sources	▪ vegetation/climate types ▪ use of natural resources ▪ soil erosion ▪ impact of technology ▪ atlas/maps ▪ secondary sources	▪ water quality/quantity (pollution) ▪ weather and climate ▪ water cycle ▪ development levels ▪ IT: database ▪ diagrams/maps (OS) ▪ weather recording	▪ overview of two countries, including economic base/employment structure ▪ changes ▪ development levels/issues ▪ international trade ▪ statistics ▪ thematic maps/atlas	▪ migration patterns ▪ planning/decision making ▪ urban land use change and impact on people ▪ maps/statistics ▪ secondary sources	▪ coastal landforms and processes ▪ weathering and erosion ▪ sediment movement ▪ impact of leisure use ▪ management of valuable environments ▪ OS maps ▪ observation and recording constructing X sections, field sketches ▪ diagrams ▪ secondary sources
Scale/place	local/national (UK and EC)	national/continental/global (include USSR)	local/regional (home and EDC locality)	local, national, regional (EC and EDC: regions in EC country, 1 locality in EDC)	regional (UK home and EDC)	local/regional (UK)
Fieldwork/PFC link	organic farmer		Water Authority (local)		'Shelter' representative	coastal engineer; fieldwork
XCT Other sub.	Environmental ed. EIU / History Science	Environmental ed. EIU / Science Technology	Environmental ed. EIU / Science Technology	Citizenship Environmental ed. / EIU	Citizenship History	EIU Environmental ed. / Science

Y9

	13 Issues arising from tourism	14 Managing environments under threat	15 Large-scale energy use issues	16 Impact of manufacturing change	17 Migration issues	18 River basin management
Title						
Possible issue	Investigating the benefits and costs that tourist development brings to communities and environments	Evaluating the success of management strategies designed to protect and conserve environments under threat	How energy use can be managed to reduce environmental tests and increase quality of life	Investigating the impact of manufacturing change on the social and economic and natural environment	What causes large-scale population movements with what consequences?	Why a river basin needs managing and the resulting effects
Possible emphasis theme/skill	▪ Mediterranean vegetation and climate ▪ tourism in the EC ▪ impact of leisure on valuable environments ▪ development issues ▪ maps/atlases ▪ statistics	▪ environmental management (valuable environments) ▪ unintended effects of management ▪ global issues of environmental change ▪ future management strategies (e.g. Antarctica) ▪ secondary sources ▪ air photographs/satellite images	▪ renewable/non-renewable resources ▪ pollution tests ▪ comparative overview of USA, USSR and Japan including energy patterns trends in energy use and impact on environment ▪ IT database ▪ atlases/thematic maps	▪ distribution of manufacturing in one country ▪ changing employment structure ▪ environmental problems arising from manufacturing ▪ international trade ▪ IT database/statistics ▪ secondary sources ▪ atlases/thematic maps	▪ population structure and dynamics ▪ global patterns ▪ causes and consequences of migration ▪ overview of selected countries ▪ desertification ▪ statistics/IT ▪ diagrams ▪ maps/atlases	▪ river systems (including processes and landforms, water cycling) ▪ flooding and human response ▪ weather (anti-cyclones and depressions) ▪ water as a resource ▪ impact of technology ▪ OS maps ▪ secondary sources ▪ observation and measuring ▪ statistics
Scale/place	local, national, continental EC and EDC	national, global	national (USA/USSR/Japan)	national (USA/USSR or Japan)	regional, national, global (especially EDCS)	regional, continental
Fieldwork/PFC link	travel agent	local representatives of environmental groups scientist			Aid agency representative	fieldwork
XCT Other sub.	Citizenship EIU	Environmental ed. Citizenship / Science	EIU Environmental ed. / Technology	EIU Environmental ed. / Technology History	Citizenship History / Maths	Environmental ed. EIU / Technology Science

Figure 2

A structure for a course outline for key stage 3

Key: XCT = Cross-curricular theme. PFC = People from the community
EIU = Economic and industrial understanding. EDC = Economically developing country

Step 1   **A starting-point, including the following prior needs:**

- aims for geographical education in the school;
- the preferred approaches to teaching and learning;
- familiarity with relevant PoS and how it fits into the existing curriculum;
- some familiarity with other subjects, KS2 and cross-curricular themes.

Step 2   **Generating ideas for unit of work headings, taking into account:**

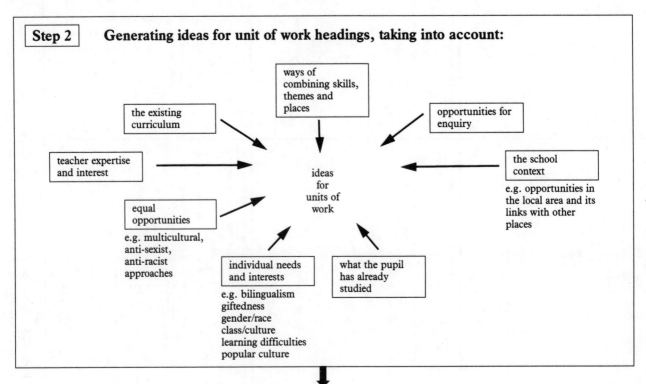

Step 3   **Noting unit emphases, including:**

- main skills, themes, places from PoS;
- other objectives, e.g. attitudes and values;
- opportunities for fieldwork and for use of people from the community.

Step 4   **Sequencing the units, taking into account:**

- progression in pupil learning;
- pattern of the year;
- timing of the fieldwork.

Step 5   **Checking and refining the course outline, including:**

- PoS and ATs;
- cross-curriculum themes;
- other subjects;
- breadth and balance (in content and learning strategies);
- availability of resources.

Step 6	Developing a broad assessment and evaluation strategy, including:

- assessment and monitoring methods;
- recording;
- pupil involvement;
- critertia for evaluation.

Figure 3: *A process for planning a key stage course outline*

Figure 3 includes a number of matters which need to be taken into account when generating the list of units. The order in which they are dealt with is immaterial. The important thing is to bear them *all* in mind, since they each have a part to play in informing choices of units of work as explained below.

The existing curriculum

The existing curriculum will be an important factor as it will determine the resources already available in addition to units, topics or teaching and learning strategies that have been successful. For example, there may be some valuable fieldwork as part of an existing topic that could be incorporated.

Combining skills, themes and places

No matter which of the three approaches is selected, it is essential to find ways of combining skills, themes and places. This can be achieved in different ways. For example, in a thematic unit about woodland and forests, the rainforest of Brazil could be used and wider knowledge of the country built up. Within this, pupils could be developing skills such as using different maps, atlases and air photographs.

Enquiry

Opportunities for enquiry are endless if an issue-based approach is selected. Otherwise, one way is to look for opportunities to include controversial issues in the study of any place or theme.

The school context

Studies of the local area and home region are required and it is worth considering exactly what the opportunities are in terms of the school environment (see Figure 4), local environment and community. Local area enquiries can be used to support both place and theme components and may be a good starting-point for any unit of work. For example, a local ecosystem, such as parkland, woodland or sand dunes might provide opportunities to develop the themes. This could include investigations of vegetation, soils, water, leisure and environmental management.

Links with other places are an excellent starting-point for the development of place and locational knowledge. Twinning arrangements or ethnic communities with strong links with the country of origin may prompt valuable ideas. There may be a large multinational company sited near the school with which links could be developed and which could act as a springboard for investigations of its role and impact in economically developing countries.

1 Compare the vegetation in two areas of the school grounds using a quadrat survey.

2 Investigate footpath erosion using a vegetation transect survey.

3 Carry out a soil survey.

4 Compare infiltration rates for different surfaces.

5 Investigate energy efficiency in the school buildings using temperature and draught measurements.

6 Study micro climates around the school grounds.

7 Measure the pollution levels in the school environment.

8 Develope or evaluate a plan to improve an area of the school grounds.

9 Investigate a small-scale ecosystem in the school grounds (e.g. hedgerow, pond, wooded copse, field, etc.).

10 Devise a trail in the school environment by drawing a map and fieldsketches and planning a route.

Figure 4: *Ten uses of the school environment*

A note about scale

The programmes of study specify study of place at two scales: localities and regions. The geography Working Group attempted to clarify this. In relation to the home area and region, it suggests that locality is the immediate vicinity of the school or home or both, 'up to a few miles away' (DES, 1990, p.13). Home region, however, is seen to be 'an area which is substantial either in size or population, e.g. N.E. England, E. Anglia, or Greater London and its surroundings' (op. cit., p. 61). They recognised this would be a subjective decision on the part of teachers.

What the pupil has already studied

If the pupils are to develop their understanding, skills and values in geography without major gaps or overlaps, consideration must be made of what the pupils have already studied and the teaching and learning approaches they have experienced. So, for example, if a local shopping study is done in KS2 a different focus for local studies is probably needed in KS3.

Individual needs

If all pupils are going to be interested, stimulated and experience positive achievement it is vital to take individual needs and interests into account. Taking the example of gender, it is important to ensure units are 'girl-friendly' as well as 'boy-friendly'. Girls may not be as motivated as boys by an enquiry into the re-siting of a football ground. However, an enquiry into the development of a new hospital or 'trendy clothing' manufacturers would probably interest more of both sexes.

Equal opportunities

Planning for equal opportunities is closely linked with the last point but warrants a separate mention. If, for example, racism is to be tackled in the teaching programme, opportunities for developing understanding, empathy and respect for people of races other than the pupil's own must be developed. An example might be a unit on migration which aims to dispel some of the myths about the origins of the black communities in Britain, balancing this with an investigation of white migration.

Teacher expertise and interest

Finally, decisions should also be informed by particular expertise amongst the teachers in a department. A teacher who has travelled widely could make an important input to the planning of a unit which focuses on a particular place. An expert on green issues might suggest a unit on an environmental issue.

Step 3: Noting unit emphases

Once the list of units has been drafted some thought needs to be given to the objectives and emphases of each one. The objectives and emphases could include a breakdown of important knowledge and understanding, skills, and values and attitudes to be covered. Many of these would relate to the requirements of the geography Order. In addition, opportunities for fieldwork and links with people from the community should be noted. Examples of what this might look like can be found in the example course outline plan (Figure 2).

Step 4: Sequencing the units

In order to decide the order of the units a key stage planner would be useful, in which the pattern of the year can be seen at a glance. This enables the timings of units to be seen as well as the periods in a school year which can disrupt the teaching programme (e.g. the build-up to Christmas or the end of the summer term).

Progression

It is crucial to take account of progression in order to build on what the pupils have learnt already. This is not an easy task for teachers when pupils develop at different rates and in reality all classes are mixed-ability. Nevertheless, it will be obvious in some cases that certain units need to come before others in order to build up the experiences and learning of all pupils. An example can be taken from the course outline in Figure 2 where 'Conflict in a local ecosystem' comes before 'Pressure on large-scale ecosystems'. This allows for progression in all the areas suggested by the geography Working Group, as shown in the list below.

Progression in the study of ecosystems in key stage 3
(see Figure 2 for unit summaries)

breadth	ecosystem study extends to different environments and places;
scale	moves from small scale in the locality to the national and international scales;
complexity	the issue takes on more dimensions as the scale of the ecosystem extends;
abstraction	as the issue moves away from an ecosystem which the pupils know and can visit, the level of abstract thinking increases;
precision	a larger-scale, more complex issue requires increased depth and precision of analysis, synthesis and evaluation;
awareness and understanding of issues	widening awareness of different ecosystem issues and deeper understanding of the complexities of issues relating to ecosystems.

(Areas of progression taken from DES, 1990, p.12)

It might also be helpful to look at how progression is built into the attainment targets. An example is given in the *Non-statutory Guidance* of the progression of statements relating to rivers and river basins (NCC, 1991, p.C12). Also in this document the statements for each attainment target are grouped in a table which enables you to see at a glance any obvious progression in the levels. Again this may suggest an order to some of the units.

Other considerations

Care also needs to be taken to ensure that pupils in KS3 who are new to the school are given an induction to ways of working with their geography teachers. It is important to take into account what the pupils studied immediately before moving school. Also in KS3 the emphasis in place is on the home region whereas in KS2 it is the local area so an early unit should help pupils identify the home region. This would offer possibilities for fieldwork. It would be helpful to think about the best times of the year for fieldwork when placing the other units with major fieldwork elements.

Step 5: Checking and refining the draft outline

In order to ensure National Curriculum requirements are being met and there is an overall coherence and balance to the key stage teaching programme a number of checks are needed.

National Curriculum for geography key stage requirements

The course outline can be checked against the key stage programme of study emphases (Resource 1) or against the details of the programme of study itself. It may also be useful to check against statements of attainment at the appropriate levels using the tables in the *Non-statutory Guidance* (NCC, 1991, pp.B3–B14). As a general rule and wherever possible 'individual statements of attainment should be covered in more than one unit of work' (op. cit., p.C8). This allows pupils at least two opportunities to achieve that statement as well as reinforcing their learning, though it may not always be practical.

Contributions to the cross-curricular elements

This is a good time to attempt to identify the contributions of the course outline to the cross-curricular elements. Curriculum Guidance 3, *The Whole Curriculum* provides a summary of the requirements of the Dimensions, Skills and Themes (NCC, 1990a, pp.2–6).

Geography has the potential to contribute to all the Themes, though it has a particular role in environmental education, economic and industrial understanding[1] and citizenship. Not least is its use of the process for enquiry which encourages active involvement in decision making and the thinking through of possible actions to be taken. These are obvious requirements for taking on the role of citizen and exploring issues relating to citizenship, the economy and industry, and the environment.

For each of the three Themes suggested it would be a good idea to refer to the aims and objectives of the document, identify where in the course outline a contribution is made, and consider where the contribution could be increased. The process of doing this may suggest a change of emphasis in some units.

Breadth and balance

Checking breadth and balance involves ensuring that the outline includes a broad range and balance of:

- places and topics or issues;
- teaching and learning strategies.

Scale / Unit										
LOCAL	local area (school and/or home)									
	contrasting UK locality									
	EC locality beyond the UK									
	ED locality									
REGIONAL	home region									
	two regions in an EC country									
	other									
NATIONAL	USA, Japan or USSR									
	ED country									
	EC country									
GLOBAL (including Continental and International)										

Now underline, using different colours, places from the Eastern (formerly Communist block), those from the West and those from economically developing areas of the world.

Resource 2: *A scale coverage matrix*   Key: ED = economically developing; EC = European community

1   See Geography, Schools and Industry Project (GSIP) publications by Graham Corney, 1991.

An important way of achieving breadth and balance of places is by ensuring those studied are from a range of political, cultural, ethnic and economic systems. This would include both places from other countries and those in England and Wales. For example, it would be very easy to omit any enquiry into places where ethnic communities live if your school is in a predominantly white area. Breadth and balance can also be achieved by including a variety of spatial scales from local to global. Resource 2 provides a list for checking the breadth and balance of scale and place.

Providing breadth and balance in teaching and learning strategies will help pupils develop different skills and have a range of learning experiences. It is important to bear in mind that enquiry should be incorporated and the course outline should be checked to ensure opportunities are there.

Availability of resources

It was suggested that existing resources be taken into account when generating unit headings. When checking the outline it would be useful to consider resources again by answering these questions:

1 What existing resources can be used again?

2 What resources are needed?
   - which will have to be purchased?
   - are any freely available?
   - which could be made?

3 How will resources be used?

It may be that in the light of this units need adapting because the resources needed are not feasible. One of the concerns of teachers and especially heads of department is how they will resource the National Curriculum. It has been emphasised that wherever possible existing resources are utilised or adapted. Figure 5 provides a checklist of some resources which should be useful when implementing the National Curriculum. These may well be priorities when deciding what is needed. Sharing with other subjects would be feasible in some cases.

Fieldwork equipment	compasses, clinometers, tape measures, ranging poles, quadrats, soil testing kit.
Weather instruments	maximum–minimum thermometer, rain guage, anemometer, wind vane, barograph (some of these could be borrowed or home-made).
IT	databases, data handling packages, simulations/models.

Maps	globe, copies of different map projections, maps of the local area and home region (e.g. OS 1:50,000, 1:25,000, 1:10,000, 1:2,500, street maps, tourist maps).
Photographs/images	aerial photographs of the local area, satellite images showing weather and places to be studied, photographs of distant places to be studied (see pp.46–47).
Information about places	information from the local planning department on major proposals for change in the local area/home region, tourist information, authentic information from people who live in distant places (see p.47).
Information about topical issues	newspaper cuttings, TV news clips/documentaries, information from pressure groups, industries, planning departments, developers.

Figure 5: *Some useful resources for the National Curriculum for geography*

Once the KS3 course outline is in place the same procedure should be used for KS4. In this case you will need to work within the guidelines for KS4 geography and the GCSE syllabus if appropriate.

Step 6: Developing a broad assessment and evaluation strategy

Once the course outlines have been refined it is important to pay some attention to how the pupils will be assessed, how their progress will be monitored, and how this will be recorded. At this stage departmental policy along broad lines should be agreed rather than planned in detail. School policy on assessment and recording will no doubt inform teachers' thinking on this.

A note about assessment in the National Curriculum

In the National Curriculum two forms of assessment are to be used to measure pupils' achievements in relation to the ten levels of attainment within each attainment target:

1 Teacher Assessment Tasks (TATs) which are ways of collecting evidence and making judgements integrated into normal patterns of teaching and learning;

2 Standard Assessment Tasks (SATs) which are the end of key stage tasks set nationally but with a bank of tasks for teachers to choose from. (In the case of KS4 this procedure will only be used in non-GCSE courses.)

The idea is that standards will be safeguarded by comparisons between results of the two methods and with the judgements of other teachers.

Since TATs are the teachers' responsibility you will need to develop a policy about them. It is important to bear in mind the principles of TATs which are:

1 They are formative in purpose, i.e. they are part of a continuous process of monitoring pupils' progress and setting goals for the future;

2 They are an integral part of teaching and learning and not a separate activity using extra tasks or tests;

3 Pupils should be actively involved in the process in order to be aware of their progress, achievements and future goals.

These principles have been gleaned from the Secondary Examinations and Assessment Council's (SEAC's) broadsheet, *Teacher Assessment at Key Stage 3* (1991). They also stress that evidence of attainment can be in many forms including the less formal teacher observation and questioning.

Since there is no nationally prescribed system, a method of recording attainment is needed. This could be in the form of a profile or record of achievement and it may be that the school has a common policy on this.

Finally, it would be useful to consider how the success of this new curriculum will be evaluated. Below is a list of example criteria that a department could use at a later date for evaluation.

Evaluation criteria for a course outline

- Was there a coherence to each unit?

- Were pupils able to build on the skills and understanding of previous units?

- Did pupils develop their attitudes and values through successive units?

- Are pupils enjoying and involved in the learning programme?

- Are all pupils achieving positively within their ability?

Conclusion

This is a very important stage in planning since the course outline will set the tone of the entire key stage curriculum. In this chapter it has been suggested that teachers can use a logical method to plan a course outline. This method enables teachers to organise and subdivide the relevant programme of study into a meaningful and coherent teaching and learning programme. A step-by-step approach has been described which starts from the philosophy of the teacher and the existing curriculum as well as the National Curriculum requirements.

Q **Tasks**

Try following the step-by-step approach to planning a course outline illustrated in Figure 3 for KS3. Try to ensure that you take account of all the suggestions. At each step in the planning you might like to include the following tasks.

- **Step 1** Discuss the relative value of taking a place, thematic or issue-based approach to units of work. Consider any advantages or disadvantages of a combination of approaches.

- **Step 2** Consider the opportunities offered by the environment local to the school (within a few miles). For example:
    - school grounds (see Figure 4);
    - different land uses;
    - change and conflict in land use;
    - businesses and services for potential links;
    - people from the community (e.g. community leaders, planners, trades union officials, parents, interest group representative);
    - more natural environments (e.g. river, coast, woodland, parkland).

- **Step 3** For each of the units discuss the opportunities for fieldwork and links with people from the community. Refer to ideas in the last task and consider ways of linking with people from more distant communities.

- **Step 4** Discuss your ideas about planning for progression. Taking this into account, sequence the units. Use a course planning matrix similar to the one in Figure 2.

- **Step 5**

    1 Use the matrix in Resource 2 to check the breadth and balance of scale and place covered in your course outline.
      a) For each unit tick and/or make a note of the scales/places to be studied in the relevant box.
      b) Check the balance of places from economically developing countries, the 'Eastern' (formerly Communist) block and 'Western' countries. Use three colours to underline these different types. Consider any possible refinements as a result of this review.

    2 For each unit identify what, if any, link there may be with other subjects and cross-curricular themes.

    Now complete the course outline planning matrix with any refinements you have made.

- **Step 6**

    a) Refer to the principles of TATs (Step 6 in the text). Discuss and generate a departmental policy on assessing and recording pupil achievement. How might pupils be involved in the process?
    b) Devise a set of criteria for evaluating the course outline. (See the example in the box on p.26.)

5 Planning units of work and lesson sequences

The purpose of this stage in planning is to develop a sequence of lesson summaries for each unit heading in the key stage course outline. This planning can be done gradually, as the implementation timetable progresses.

In this chapter there is, firstly, an overview of the process of planning a unit of work; secondly, a look at the enquiry process and how it can be used in planning; and thirdly, examples of lesson sequences planned using the enquiry process.

The process of planning a unit of work

Any unit will be made up of a certain number of lessons (unless it involves off-timetable fieldwork). It could either be organised as one sequence of lessons or it may naturally subdivide into two or more sequences. A sequence of lessons simply involves organising the study of a particular topic or issue into manageable parts (i.e. a number of lessons). The planning process suggested in this chapter can be applied to any of the three approaches (theme, place or issue-based), and is summarised in Figure 6.

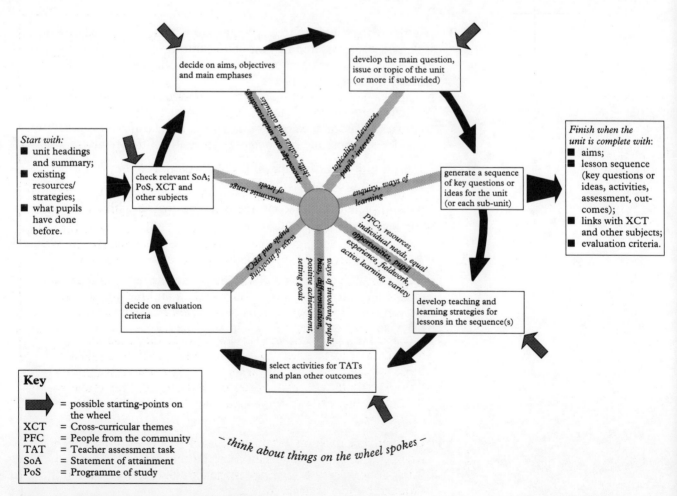

Figure 6: *A planning wheel for units of work*

A starting point

Some of the groundwork for the unit will already have been done at the course outline planning stage. In order to start unit planning at least a heading or summary is needed for each unit in the outline. Any existing resources, strategies or schemes of work should feed into the planning as well as what the pupils have already studied.

The planning wheel

This 'wheel' summarises a process for planning units of work. It can be joined at a number of places according to teachers' preferred ways of working. Nevertheless, it is necessary to cover the entire wheel in the direction of the arrows, repeating this until the plan is satisfactory. A planning matrix (such as the ones shown in the example units in Figures 7 and 8 or the blank matrix in Resource 3) can be completed as the process is followed. One method of using the wheel is described below. It starts by checking National Curriculum requirements.

Unit _____

Key question/topic/issue _____ Emphases _____

KS _____ Year _____

Lesson	Sequence of key ideas or questions	Learning activities including fieldwork and assessment	Resources/PFC	Main SoAs	Cross-curricular theme	Other subjects

Resource 3: *Matrix for planning a unit of work or sequence of lessons*

One way of using the planning wheel (Figure 6)

1 Identify statements of attainment and components of the programme of study and cross-curricular themes relevant to the unit heading and summary. This ensures familiarity with the requirements. It is important to make sure there is a spread of levels to ensure pupils of all abilities can achieve positively.

2 Refine the objectives and emphases of the unit as generated at the course outline planning stage. These may include non-statutory elements, for example the development of values.

3 Decide whether the unit needs subdividing into different lesson sequences. Then develop the main question, issue or topic for each sequence. Both topicality (e.g. the possibility of linking the unit to topical issues in the news) and relevance to the pupils (e.g. linking with their interests) should be considered.

4 Generate the most important key idea or key question for each lesson in the sequence. When deciding the order of lessons think about ways of learning (especially the enquiry process) in order to build a logical sequence.

5 Develop a variety of teaching and learning strategies which will help pupils understand the key idea or answer the question posed in each lesson. It is important to consider individual needs and ways of linking with the pupils' own experience. There may be strategies and resources already in existence that can be used again. There may also be opportunities for linking with people from the community and developing fieldwork.

6 Identify which of the activities planned would provide evidence that a pupil had achieved a statement of attainment (this can form a TAT) and any other outcomes. Examples of TATs or other outcomes could include: a display for parents, a letter to a local newspaper or an anotated map. Care should be taken to avoid potential bias in TATs in order to give all pupils the opportunity to achieve (e.g. wording of tasks, too much emphasis on written communication, taking account of bilingualism). It may be necessary to rethink teaching and learning strategies in the light of this. If so, go back to No. 5.

7 Consider how the unit will be evaluated and how pupils and people from the community could be involved.

8 Check the programme of study, statements of attainment and cross-curricular themes again to ensure requirements are being met and to look for opportunities to develop them further.

Go round the wheel again in order to make refinements.

Another method of using the planning wheel is to start with teaching and learning strategies. This may be the case if, for example, there is a high degree of underachievement and disaffection amongst pupils. In this case the top priority may be to plan activities designed to interest and motivate them.

Enquiry learning

As mentioned in Chapter 3, it is a requirement of the geography Order that an enquiry approach is incorporated into the teaching programme. This is an approach which is used widely by geography teachers partly because of the influence of a number of curriculum development projects (e.g. GYSL, Geography 14 to 18, Geography 16 to 19 Project and GSIP). There are opportunities to build enquiry into lesson sequences and units of work which are described in this section.

A definition of enquiry learning

In its widest sense, enquiry learning is when pupils are actively enquiring into things, i.e. asking questions, seeking information or solving problems, rather than simply soaking in the information and ideas of another person. Enquiry learning is usually associated with a series of stages which are passed through in order to investigate an issue, problem or question. This is usually referred to as the 'enquiry process' (in the case of GSIP) or 'route to enquiry' (in the case of the 16 to 19 Project) with a sequence of questions to guide pupil learning through the stages (see Figure 7). This process or route was also suggested by the geography Working Group as outlined in Chapter 3.

Stage of enquiry	Sequence of questions	Learning activities	Statement of attainment
1 Gain awareness	What is the issue? Who is effected? What do I feel about it?	Watch news clip (Bangladesh village flooded). Group discussion to share ideas and feelings about the situation these people are in.	AT1 4e
2 Define and describe	Where is this village? What is the village and surrounding environment like? What do the people do? What is the river system normally like? What was the extent of the flood? How did it effect this place? How does this village fit into the river basin?	Use variety of resources to find out and <u>display what this place is like and where it is</u> (e.g. atlas, maps, photos, air photos, climate graph, interviews). <u>Annotate a map of the river basin.</u> Use air photos/satellite images to find out the extent of flooding at local and national scale. In groups construct an annual hydrograph and rainfall graph and a graph of sediment levels.	AT1 3d, 7c AT2 3d, 4e, 5c, 6c AT3 4c, 6d.
Analyse and explain	Why do people live here? What caused the flood? How has the river system changed over time? How do changes that people make to the land in other places affect this place?	Creative writing summarising views of villagers about the benefits of living here and how they responded to the flood. <u>Sequence and annotate a set of diagrams to show the consequences of deforestation in the mountain region of the river basin.</u> Either <u>write a report or draw a spider diagram to explain the factors causing the flood.</u>	as above plus: AT3 4b, 7b, 7d
3 Predict Make decisions	How can flooding be reduced? What proposals are there? What is the likely management strategy? What impact will it have on land and people?	Groups research and design a management scheme for the mts. to reduce flooding downstream. Present and justify. Expert (e.g. technology teacher) evaluates schemes. <u>Costs and benefits of each scheme listed and most likely scheme selected.</u>	AT5 4C, 6c, 7a
Evaluate and respond personally	Have my feelings towards people of the Bangladeshi village changed? How? What do I think should happen? What important things did I learn from this investigation?	<u>Review the investigation</u> e.g. what you have learnt about disasters and peoples' responses to them; how your feelings have changed; what you believe should happen now in Bangladesh. Make up your own list of principles for managing environmental disasters (option of selecting from a teacher-provided list).	AT3 5c, 6g (and any of above)

Figure 7: *How can flooding in Bangladesh be managed? An example sequence of lessons planned using the enquiry process (underlined activities are those aimed at assessing pupil achievement in relation to SoAs)*

Ways of using the enquiry process in unit planning

This process can be used in a number of ways:

1 as a structure for the teacher in planning a sequence of lessons;

2 as a structure for the teacher in planning a small-scale activity, e.g. a decision-making exercise or a problem-solving task;

3 as a structure for pupils undertaking an independent or group investigation;

4 part of the process used in planning an activity, lesson or sequence of lessons.

Using the enquiry process to plan units of work and lesson sequences can be achieved by developing key questions and learning activities which relate to the stages of the enquiry process. This method is suggested by GSIP (see Corney and GSIP teachers, 1991; Corney, 1991).

Of the other ways of using enquiry, the one using only part of the enquiry process (No. 4) is perhaps least satisfactory. This is because each stage of the enquiry process is crucial in the learning process, especially the last one where pupils make sense of the new information for themselves.

With all four suggestions the pupil can have differing amounts of responsibility for control of the process. For example, if the teacher uses the process to plan a sequence of lessons there is no reason why pupils cannot have a say in what questions they should be asking or what data they need.

Progression in enquiry learning

Progression can occur in the amount of responsibility the pupils have in directing enquiries. In KS4, pupils are expected to have more independence by undertaking an individual or group enquiry. The process of taking on more responsibility should be gradual and start before KS4.

The conclusions of the geography Working Group are helpful when considering progression. They listed enquiry activities for pupils in each key stage (DES 1990, pp.59, 68). In this they implied the following types of progression:

- from suggesting enquiry questions to formulating them;
- from making some contributions to enquiry planning to taking full responsibility;
- from systematic to accurate field observation (data collection);
- from identifying and describing to analysing resulting patterns and relationships;
- from drawing careful conclusions to those supported by evidence and sound reasoning;
- increasing the quality of the structure and organisation of enquiry findings;
- from using the experience to identify changes in personal beliefs to questioning or changing of personal attitudes and values.

Examples of lesson sequences for KS3 units

In the following examples the enquiry process is incorporated into the planning of lesson sequences using the method suggested by GSIP (Corney and GSIP, 1991; Corney, 1991). Summaries of the examples are given in Figures 7 and 8.

Example 1: Flooding in Bangladesh

Figure 7 provides the first example of a sequence of lessons. This sequence would form the major part of Unit 18 in the example course outline (Figure 2) and contains about nine hours' teaching time plus homework.

	Enquiry process	Enquiry questions	Learning activities	Statement of attainment
Lesson sequence 1	Gain awareness	What is the weather like around the school campus?	Carry out a perception study of the micro climate of the school campus.	AT3 4a
	Define/describe	Where do you go to get out of the rain or wind? Which parts of the school campus are most sheltered and which get the most sunshine?	Pupils prepare choropleth map to show warmest, coldest and windiest places. Record wind speeds around the school campus using hand-made and commercially-produced anemometers. Choropleth the results.	AT1 4d, 6e
	Analyse/explain	Why are some parts of the school grounds windier than others? How do the school buildings influence the wind strength and direction?	Describe and explain the results in terms of prevailing winds and turbulence around buildings.	AT3 4a
	Make decision Evaluate	Where would be the most suitable site on the school campus for a small-scale wind-powered generator?	Using a landscape sketch and BWEA advice on how to site a small wind turbine, choose the best location and explain the choice.	AT3 4a
Lesson sequence 2	Gain awareness Define/describe Analyse/explain	Where would be the most suitable site in a local area of Mid Wales for the location of a wind farm?	Collection of specific information from free literature on wind energy (from BWEA, British aerospace) e.g. location of test turbines in UK, global location of wind farms.	AT4 4e
	Predict	What would be the implications of a wind farm on the local environment? What impact would the wind farm have on the global environment? How might the local economy be affected?	Analyse 1:50,000 map of the Dovey Estuary to find suitable location for wind farm (considering topography, proximity of Snowdonia National Park, and conflict with any other existing land use).	AT1 5b, 6b; AT4 4e
	Make decision	Who might object to such a development and why? What would the tourists think? What about the local farmers or businesses?	Sorting and ranking letters received by Montgomery District Council both in support and objecting to the Dovey Valley wind farm. Writing of letter to local MP either for or against the scheme.	AT2 6a AT4 4e AT5 5b, 6a
	Evaluation Personal response	How can we make the most of the energy resources we have?	Production of flier for public distribution either for or against the wind farm synthesising all information collected.	AT2 4c, 6a, 7a AT4 4e, AT5 5a, 6a, 7a

Figure 8: *Unit of work on wind energy*   Key: BWEA = British Wind Energy Association

The main question being addressed by the sequence is: 'how can flooding in Bangladesh be managed?' The first stage in the process involves pupils looking at a recent flood disaster in Bangladesh. This is seen to be a good starting-point since an issue that pupils hear about in the news is more likely to grab their interest. Also, seeing how families and individuals in one village have been affected makes the issue more personal. Therefore pupils may identify with the people, particularly if girls and boys of their own age are shown.

In the second stage of the enquiry process, pupils are asked to think about information in relation to this issue. This is achieved by pupils describing and analysing the disaster in both the village and whole river basin context. Stereotypical and negative images of the villagers could be counteracted here by emphasising positive aspects of the villagers' lifestyle and describing the ways they are dealing with problems themselves.

The final stage is concerned with the pupils making sense of the information for themselves by developing their own management solutions to the flood hazard and evaluating the alternatives. During this an 'expert' is present as a consultant for the pupils, who evaluates their ideas for flood management. This could be an environmental manager or a technology teacher.

As personal responses to the issue pupils are asked to draw up their own principles for environmental management. To do this involves a sound grasp of the ideas in this lesson sequence and the development or clarification of values.

The ways in which evidence of achievement would be collected and judged are shown on the matrix of Figure 7 by underlined activities. Notice the variety of assessment methods giving different ways for pupils to communicate their understanding or demonstrate their skills (report writing, anotating a map and diagram, constructing a spider diagram, making a display). The range of levels that could be attained in this sequence (3–7) allows for pupils of differing abilities to achieve positively.

Example 2: Wind energy

Recently, a National Curriculum unit of work on wind energy was piloted at Llandrindod Wells High School. This unit of work was planned for a mixed-ability Y8 group with a total of about twelve hours' teacher contact time plus a day's field visit. The teacher was keen to develop a unit of work on an increasingly contentious issue in Mid Wales. Several proposals to build wind farms here of between 24 and 100 wind turbines had been made in the last eighteen months, the majority of which were opposed by landscape conservationists.

Linking with other subjects and cross-curriculum themes

In the case of this unit the original idea was conceived and researched (using National Curriculum subject and theme documents) by the teacher before any colleagues were approached. This was because the topic of wind energy was seen to be 'geography driven'. Wind energy was chosen primarily because an enquiry unit on this topic would contribute to learning about the weather, energy and environment, all of which feature in the geography programme of study for this key stage and some of which feature in science and technology. It was therefore clear that the unit could lead to close inter-departmental co-operation, in addition to contributing to the cross-curricular themes, most notably economic and industrial understanding (EIU); for example:

- visits to local manufacturers of wind turbines;
- simulation of a public enquiry into the Dovey Valley wind farm application;
- pupils taking on the role of consultants in selecting the best site for a prototype turbine in the school grounds;
- consideration of the wider economic costs and benefits of energy production.

Much of the detailed planning was carried out in separate departments though the following points were agreed by the subject teachers involved.

1 The majority of the topic would be taught in discrete subject areas with individual units of work ensuring lessons complemented rather than overlapped each other.

2 Some unifying activities would be carried out in order that the pupils recognised the holistic nature of their work. These included:

- site visits (e.g. to the Centre for Alternative Technology in Machynlleth);

- a consultation process between the geography and CDT departments, who would work in partnership in the assessment of the school site for a wind turbine.

The geography unit

Details of the geography unit and its learning activities are given in Figure 8. The unit falls into two distinct and logical enquiry sequences:

1 determining a site for a wind turbine in the school grounds;

2 investigating the environmental impact of the proposed Dovey Valley wind farm.

It is felt that the unit provided an easily understood way into the potentially dry and difficult topic of micro climates, whilst developing pupils' knowledge and understanding of wind energy, the local area and the home region. In addition the topical nature of the issue of siting a wind farm in Mid Wales proved to motivate many pupils. (For information on how this unit was assessed see p.53.)

Conclusion

In this chapter an approach has been suggested for planning units of work (shown in the planning wheel, Figure 6). This is intended to be a flexible approach since it allows a choice of where to start, according to preferred ways of working and school circumstances.

This chapter has also demonstrated how the enquiry process can be built into planning the lesson sequences which make up units of work. It is justified as a way of motivating pupils and helping them to learn effectively. Effective learning is promoted because a logical route to learning is provided in the process. Also, because pupils are actively involved in lessons they are more likely to be motivated. At the same time requirements of both the geography Order and the wider National Curriculum can be satisfied by using the enquiry approach.

Q **Tasks**

1 Refer to:

- the planning wheel (Figure 6);

- the steps suggested in the box on pp.29–30;

- the example enquiry sequence (Figure 7);

- your own course outline.

Try planning a unit using the approach shown on the planning wheel and using the enquiry process to sequence learning. Start with the box which asks you to check National Curriculum documents. (You may find it helpful to follow the steps on pp. 29–30, each of which relates to a box on the planning wheel.)

Record your plans on a planning matrix of your own (or on Resource 3).

2   As a group, discuss:

   a) what you consider enquiry learning to involve?

   b) what value it has for the 11 to 16 age range?

Decide how enquiry learning will be incorporated into your 11 to 16 geography curriculum.

6 Developing and implementing classroom ideas

This chapter is devoted to the final stages of planning the National Curriculum for geography. Once the course outline and units of work are agreed the remaining task is to plan in detail for individual lessons. Teachers are 'expert' at this, so the purpose of this chapter is not to revise lesson-planning techniques. Specific elements of detailed planning will be considered, including: individual needs, teaching and learning strategies, and assessment and evaluation.

Individual needs

Within any geography class there is bound to be a range of abilities, skills, cultural backgrounds, personalities, experiences and interests. There is no point in planning for the 'average pupil' when no such pupil exists! With the National Curriculum there are fixed outcomes expected of pupils. This means planning for individual needs is even more important since pupils may require different routes and stimuli to be able to achieve these outcomes.

Ability

Learning difficulties

For some pupils failure can be the norm, especially if they have learning difficulties. For such pupils it is important to remember that their difficulties will be unique and that it is preferable to look for what they can do. Only by passing records on, getting to know the particular pupil and liaising with specialist staff can teachers attempt to meet their needs. Above all, planned learning activities should be appropriate and relevant to the pupil whilst attempting to meet National Curriculum requirements, unless the pupil is 'disapplied' from the National Curriculum. The most common difficulties such pupils face are with reading and writing. Geography teachers have a great advantage in the variety of communication they can use in teaching and learning strategies (e.g. maps, diagrams, photographs). Good use can also be made of IT, especially word-processing facilities.

Pupils with learning difficulties will probably not achieve more than a particular level. It is therefore important to provide a stimulating experience by developing skills and understanding in different contexts (e.g. studying different places, issues, topics). Also, providing opportunities for positive achievement, not necessarily related to the levels in the National Curriculum, is vital. Teachers should seek support from specialists within the school for help and advice on planning for pupils with learning difficulties.

Planning question	Example topic: tourism in Spain (KS4, Y10)
1 What PoS requirements link to this topic?	Locality in Spain (jobs, land use, settlement, environment, location, past and present changes); tourism theme; Mediterranean vegetation and climate; change in towns/cities; location of economic activities.
2 What are the learning objectives for this lesson?	Knowledge and understanding: what this place is like (vegetation and climate, landscape, size, buildings, changes); why people go on holiday; what jobs there are. Skills: selecting, displaying and interpreting information from travel brochures (including text, tables of costs, photos, maps, climate graphs) and an atlas; summarising findings.
3 What does the pupil already know and feel about this and what can he or she already do?	He or she has been on holiday to a similar resort in Spain. He or she can find places in an atlas and is good at photograph interpretation.
4 How will the objectives be achieved? (pupil tasks, teacher's/classroom assistant's role) What content and strategies will interest the pupil?	1 Tell the classroom assistant what you liked about your holiday in Spain. Find the resort you went to and the one being studied in the atlas. 2 Cut out information about this resort from the brochures and stick on a large card with labels. 3 Fill in the resort profile and evaluation sheet provided (simple questionnaire style) with the assistant's help. 4 Discuss which of the two resorts you prefer and why.
5 What resources will be needed? Can any existing resources be modified? (e.g. the language simplified)	Travel brochures, atlas, sheet of card, glue, classroom assistant's prompt for task 1, questionnaire (including cartoons/pictures to help understanding of the questions).
6 What will the outcomes be?	Resort display, completed resort profile and evaluation to add to the display.
7 How will achievement in relation to SoAs be monitored, assessed and recorded?	Resort profile and evaluation assessed and used as evidence for achievement of any of the following SoAs: AT2 4a, 5c, 7d; AT4 4b, 5b, 5c.

Figure 9: *Questions to ask when planning for pupils with learning difficulties and an example lesson summary for a Y10 girl*

Figure 9 gives a suggested method for planning for pupils with learning difficulties and provides an example of an eighty-minute lesson for a Y10 girl. The planning method includes the use of a sequence of seven questions. The questions start with a reminder of the relevant section of the programme of study and go on to ask about the learning objectives for the lesson. These need to be appropriate to the pupil's ability and focus on what he or she will be able to achieve. The next question considers what the pupil has done before in order to build on what he or she can do.

Once the answers to these questions are established it is possible to decide on the best learning activities to achieve the objectives. There is an obvious need to provide a stimulating experience and outcomes that the pupil can be proud of. At this stage it would be a good idea to consider the classroom assistant's role (if one is available), though the pupil clearly needs opportunities to work independently or with peers. The question about resources is a crucial one since existing resources are often too difficult for pupils with learning difficulties. It may be that simple modifications to worksheets – e.g. making the language more appropriate – are all that is needed. The final questions relate to the outcomes of the lesson and how they will be assessed. Again, it may be a good idea not to rely too heavily on written outcomes unless there is a tight structure to the task.

The example lesson in Figure 9 is the start of an investigation into the impact of tourism on a small resort in Mediterranean Spain. It attempts to build on the pupil's own experience of a holiday in a similar resort. Use is made of travel brochures in an attempt to provide a stimulus and develop skills that the pupil may need in adult life. The written task is done using a highly structured and illustrated questionnaire. The pupil has to make use of information in the travel brochure and his or her own holiday in order to answer the questions. These questions give the pupil the opportunity to achieve a number of statements of attainment. Working towards a colourful display about this resort is seen to be an added stimulus for the pupil. The example given would need to be modified for a pupil who had never been abroad. Nevertheless, they would still have images of holidays in Spain which could be used.

Exceptional ability

Within either key stage pupils with exceptional ability could be working towards the highest levels and in the case of KS3 to levels beyond the expected range. Alternative or extension activities and more sophisticated resources can be used to stretch these pupils further. It is important to provide a variety of challenges and not just further written work. A list of possible ideas is provided below. These ideas could be useful for any pupil.

Possible activities for exceptionally able pupils

Exceptionally able pupils could be asked to:

- do some further research on the topic or issue being investigated using reference books in the library or databases in the IT room;

- write for a critical audience (e.g. *New Scientist* or *The Guardian*) or write a letter to one of these;

- take part in and tape record a discussion or debate as a pair, each taking a different viewpoint (use an empty room or office);

- present a piece of work to their year head, deputy head, or another geography teacher and explain it to them;

- discuss and evaluate a piece of their work with an 'expert' who is present in the classroom (e.g. planner, business person, conservationist);

- develop a resource for teaching pupils about this topic in future years (e.g. a video, information sheet, game);

- take an existing resource and improve it (e.g. new voice-over for a video);

- undertake an ongoing weather project using the school's satellite system.

The ideas of the geography Working Group about progression (p.12 and see DES, 1990, p.12) could be used to determine the way in which skills and understanding could be developed further for able pupils.

Mixed-ability teaching

With such a wide range of ability, content, activities and resources must be adapted for pupils of different abilities within the same class. This is nothing new to experienced mixed-ability teachers. One of the new issues arising from the National Curriculum is how to cope with mixed-ability classes when content (e.g. particular places or landforms) is built in to the attainment targets. For example, in a typical mixed-ability Y9 class, pupils working at levels 3 and 4 need to study places at the local and regional scale. However, pupils working to higher levels are expected to concentrate mostly on the national scale. This suggests that teachers will have to consider alternative content and tasks within lessons. A way of planning for this when studying one country is to have pupils who are working towards higher levels investigating a topic or issue at the national scale and others doing so at the local scale (see Figure 10). This sounds daunting but all teachers of a particular year group will face the same problem so it should be possible to share the planning and resourcing of particular activities.

Enquiry questions for this lesson: What is this village and surrounding environment like? Why do people live here and what do they do?

Activity 1: all pupils

Pupils collect information about the village (before the flood) and record it by filling in a village profile form. Information is placed around the classroom and walls. Pupils circulate in pairs.

SoA: AT1 4c

Extension activity (more able pupils): Describe and explain the impact of the environment, location and wealth on the village community.

SoA AT2 4e, 5c

Resources needed for this lesson

- black and white/colour photographs of: buildings; land uses; landscape; people (daily life);
- maps and aerial photograph of the village (showing scale, services, layout of village, immediate surroundings ...);
- video or tape of interviews with villagers (or in textbook);
- simple climate graphs for this village and pupils' home region;
- photocopies of map and black and white photographs;
- a few photographs of the school's local area;
- thematic maps of Bangladesh (possibly in the atlas);
- Satellite images of Bangladesh.

Activity 2: pupils with learning difficulties

Pupils select two photographs to show daily life and features of their local area. They add a comment about surroundings and what it is like to live here using speech bubbles. This is repeated for the Bangladeshi village and displayed. The teacher or classroom assistant asks the pupils to compare the two places verbally.

SoA: AT2 3d

Activity 2: most pupils

Pupils design an A3 display about this village. They draw a map of this place and select a couple of the photographs. These are annotated to show what this place is like and why. Extra descriptions and explanations can be added if pupils want to.

SoA: AT2 4e, 5c; AT1 4f

Activity 2: more able pupils

Pupils use thematic maps and satellite images of Bangladesh. They make notes on the varying conditions in the country and relate these to the population distribution. The factors influencing population distribution here are summarised in a diagram or table. A written report is added to explain the diagram.

SoA: AT2 6c; AT1 5d, 7c

Figure 10: *A mixed-ability lesson: teaching and learning about places*

With other content (apart from place) it should be possible to differentiate between pupils of different abilities by outcome rather than task. In this way pupils can work to their own ability whilst having an equal opportunity to content material and resources.

Rights of groups

It is important to ensure that the gender, race and social class of pupils and the wider community are taken into account when planning at all levels. This plays a part in reducing the feelings of alienation that some pupils experience and so will help them to achieve their potential.

In the last ten years or so multicultural, anti-racist and anti-sexist approaches to teaching and learning have been recognised as important by many teachers. Multicultural education emphasises the development of tolerance as well as the celebration of differences between cultural groups. Anti-racist and anti-sexist approaches develop attitudes further by emphasising social injustice and its reasons, and looking at strategies to reduce inequalities and combat racism. Increasingly geography teachers have realised the potential of their subject to contribute to this. Many teachers believe that these approaches help address individual needs as well as preparing pupils for life in a multicultural society. Such approaches involve the consideration of appropriate teaching and learning strategies, content and materials when planning lessons.

Teaching and learning strategies clearly have a major part to play in determining achievement. For example, in many secondary classrooms question-and-answer sessions are dominated by boys, so ways of involving girls in talk and discussion should be considered. Research suggests that boys perform better than girls at map reading and that girls have particular difficulty with OS 1:50,000 and 1:25,000 maps (Boardman and Towner, 1979). One theory for this gender difference is that boys tend to explore a wider territory around the home than girls when growing up, so developing spatial awareness on a larger scale. The use of OS 1:2,500 street and mental maps are possible ways of enabling some girls (and boys) to develop their skills. However, since the geography Order requires the testing of OS map skills at the two larger scales mentioned, ways of building up to these from more 'friendly' maps are essential.

Content is vital since this often determines the pupil's interest. If it encompasses experience of and relevance to their own race, gender or class as well as others, pupils are more likely to become mentally involved. There are endless examples of invisibility of women or non-white race groups in the content of geography topics. Within any topic it is important to look for opportunities to include the experience of both sexes and different cultural groups. Farming, for example, is often seen to be a male domain when in reality the majority of the world's farmers are women and in many parts of the world they are the mainstay of the farming economy. For resources which aim to make women more visible see the 'Women's Lives' series available from Womankind and the journal *Contemporary Issues in Geography and Education.*

In the case of many geography textbooks and materials there is still a predominance of white men portrayed in their images of people. Women are often invisible and non-white race groups are associated with poverty and problems. This can 'switch off' girls and pupils from ethnic minorities as they may see little of relevance to their own lives. There is a need to consider ways of balancing these images, not least because positive images are more likely to engender tolerance and feelings of respect and empathy towards other groups of people. Development Education Centres stock many examples of resources aimed at providing positive images.

A note about language

Language used in the geography classroom is fundamentally important in helping pupils learn. In the case of many pupils, especially 'working class' pupils and those who do not speak English in the home, geography-speak can be very unfriendly and a barrier to learning. Some ways many geography teachers overcome this include:

- the use of non-written information, e.g. maps, diagrams, models, photographs, cartoons, videos and songs to help pupils communicate and develop their understanding;

- allowing pupils to talk in pairs and groups in order for them to make sense of ideas using their own level of language;

- scrutinising existing resources and materials for over-complexity of language (various 'readability' tests are available, though simply scanning text for difficult words and over-long sentences or sections is just as helpful).

Teaching and learning strategies

Teaching and learning strategies are the ways of working that teachers set up in order to help pupils learn. This includes both selection of activities and pupil groupings within the class. Pupil activities may range from those focused on the teacher (e.g. listening to a teacher explanation) to those centred on the pupil (e.g. designing a shopping centre). The box below gives a wide range of strategies that are currently utilised by geography teachers to differing degrees.

Examples of teaching and learning strategies

Observing: on fieldtrips, videos, photographs;

Reading: aloud, silently, fiction/non-fiction, maps, graphs, tables;

Interpreting: photographs, maps, graphs, statistics, different viewpoints;

Talking/listening: teacher exposition, visitor to the classroom, conducting a questionnaire or interview, making a tape cassette recording, asking questions of an 'expert';

Expressing opinions: creative writing e.g. poems, songs; role play, drama; debate; designing posters/wall displays; writing a newspaper report or letter; making and justifying a decision;

Writing/recording: fieldwork e.g. taking notes, fieldsketching, recording data; writing an analytical report or essay; structured questions; writing for different audiences; using a word processor;

Modelling/constructing/creating: a game, display, 3d model, diagram, graph, using a computer simulation or statistical test, devising plans or solutions to problems;

Researching: using the library or a database, a reference book or atlas.

Pupil groupings include pupils working individually or together as a whole class, in small groups or pairs. Many teachers would agree that variety both in activities and groupings within the class is essential. This provides for different ways and rates of learning; allows opportunities for pupils to learn from each other, from the teacher and by themselves; and keeps pupils' interest alive. In this section enquiry learning and teaching and learning about place will be looked at in more detail.

Enquiry learning in the classroom and outside

Resource 4 suggests some conditions needed for enquiry learning to take place. The balance is tipped to pupil-centred work and the teacher takes on the role of consultant or manager both in the classroom and during fieldwork. This is not to say that teacher exposition is redundant and there may be times when the teacher needs to talk to the whole class, for example when giving instructions, explaining a task or concept, or demonstrating a skill.

Pupils are using a wide range of resources and materials.	Pupils are encouraged to think critically and not accept anything at face value.	Pupils are able to develop and clarify their own attitudes and values.
Pupils are exploring an issue, question or problem.	A clear route for enquiry is followed.	Enquiry outcomes are determined by the pupils not the teacher.
Enquiry questions are generated by the pupils themselves.	Pupils are talking more than the teacher.	Pupils decide on the personal action they can take at the end of an enquiry.
Political and social factors are brought into the enquiry.	Classroom seating is flexible to maximise pupil-to-pupil interactions.	Attitudes and values of all the people involved in the issue are explored.
Pupils reflect and think critically about their own work and set themselves goals.	Teacher talk is questioning and challenging, not telling.	Group discussion lets pupils test out and justify ideas and challenge others.

Resource 4: *Statements suggesting 'good' enquiry teaching and learning strategies*

As explained in the previous chapter the enquiry process can be used in different ways to investigate an issue, question or problem. The two main ways are:

- sequencing lessons;

- giving pupils a structure when undertaking their own enquiry.

Figure 11 provides some appropriate questions and learning strategies for each stage of the enquiry process when it is used to sequence lessons. Asking the right questions is a vital part of the enquiry process and pupils should be increasingly involved in this skill in order to gain in confidence. Notice how fieldwork is carried out at appropriate points on the route and is integrated with classroom activity. As with all enquiry learning, pupils should be actively involved in the fieldwork wherever possible. Some examples of fieldwork strategies are given below.

Twenty fieldwork ideas

1 Interview representatives or members of the public or interest groups. Make notes, video or tape record the interview.

2 Conduct a questionnaire.

3 Take photographs, make a video or draw fieldsketches of a land or townscape or to show evidence of an impact or change.

4 Observe people at work or a manufacturing process.

5 Conduct a quadrat or transect vegetation survey, e.g. across sand dunes, in a meadow or woodland, up a hill slope, in the local park.

6 Measure footpath erosion using a transect.

7 Conduct a transect survey of a small-scale landform, e.g. beach, valley, hillslope, drumlin.

8 Take river flow and channel measurements.

9 Sample and test river or lake water for pollution.

10 Use an environmental scoring chart to compare and measure environmental quality.

11 Conduct a land-use survey.

12 Conduct a building use and age survey, e.g. on an industrial estate, in a village or city.

13 Measure noise levels using a decibel meter or descriptors.

14 Measure air pollution using home-made equipment.

15 Measure river discharge and rainfall over a period of time.

16 Conduct a visitor count at a 'honeypot' site or a shopper count at a shopping centre.

17 Conduct a car park or traffic count.

18 Collect soil samples and test moisture content, ph value, colour, texture, etc.

19 Attend a public enquiry about a proposed development.

20 Visit an exhibition of proposals for a new development and collect information from it (e.g. making notes or collecting leaflets).

The key stage 4 individual or group enquiry

When pupils are doing their KS4 enquiry (a programme of study requirement in either the short or full course) the enquiry process can be used. The group or individual decides on the questions they are asking at each stage of the process and have to be involved in data collection through fieldwork. They need to decide what sort of data is required and how to collect and analyse it. Obviously most pupils will have difficulty if they are given total independence and will continue to need at least some teacher guidance, particularly in the planning stages. For these enquiries it is probably most convenient to use problems, issues or questions in the local area related to the theme and home region requirements in the programme of study. Some examples are shown below. Obviously the opportunities will vary according to the nature of the home region. All pupils could undertake the same enquiry or alternatives could be offered.

Stage of enquiry	Possible questions	Possible activities
1 Gain awareness	What is this issue, question or problem about? What do we already know and feel about it? Why is it important? Why should we look into it?	Listening to a visitor to the classroom. Going on a fieldtrip or visit. Examining a resource (e.g. newspaper, cartoon, photograph). Watching a TV news clip. Listening to a song or poem.
2 Define and describe	What information will help us find out more? Where is this place? Who is involved? What is the nature of the question, issue or problem?	Group planning: deciding on the information needed, collecting (fieldwork) and presenting it. Finding out things from an atlas, map or plan. Summarising the issue and who is involved. Drawing a map to show the extent of the problem.
Analyse and explain	What categories of information are there? How can we sort out the information to find out what it means? What are the similarities and differences? How did it get like this? Why did it happen?	Sequencing, grouping or labelling information. Translating data into graphs or diagrams. Annotating a map or photograph. Interpreting data (e.g. statistics, maps, graphs, diagrams). Looking for bias in the data. Summarising and comparing viewpoints. Discussing and clarifying ideas and explanations.
3 Predict Make decisions	What are the alternative things that could happen next? What is likely to happen next? How might things change? What impact would this have?	Making a model/designing a flow chart. Writing a report/making a video or radio documentary. Group decision making, role play, or debate. Creative writing. Consulting with people from the community.
Evaluate and respond personally	What are the different feelings and views about this and where do mine fit in? What do I think should happen? Is there anything I can do? How can I contribute to decision making? What did I learn from this investigation? Have I changed my views and thinking about this issue, question or problem?	Writing a letter expressing a personal viewpoint. Making a display for a wider audience. Developing principles or policies. Linking with a community group. Writing a poem, story or song. Designing a poster, flier or leaflet. Presenting ideas to a local councillor.

Figure 11: *Possible questions and activities for the enquiry process*

A key stage 4 enquiry: example issues and problems

- Should a big new company be allowed to locate in this area?

- Should a block of flats be demolished?

- What impact will a reservoir have on the local environment and community?

- How should the flood hazard be managed?

- What effect has a big out-of-town shopping centre had on the local area and people?

- How will the closure of a hospital affect this community?

- What impact do people have on a woodland area?

- To what extent is a farm changing because of government policy?

- How and why is this village/suburb/housing estate changing?

Teaching and learning about distant places

One part of the learning sequence in the unit of work on flooding in Bangladesh (Figure 7) related to getting to know a village and how it had been affected by the flood. Questions asked at this stage of the enquiry process included:

- Where is this village?
- What is the village and its surrounding environment like?
- What do the people do?

and later...

- Why do people live here?
- How did this flood and other ones affect these people and their environment?

Slightly modified, these questions could be used when teaching about any distant place. In his recent paper on teaching about place, Andy Owen suggests a string of questions to demonstrate what the 'knowledge of a place actually entails':

- *Where is this place?*
- *What is it like?*
- *Why is it like that?*
- *How has it changed or how might it change in the future?*
- *What would the consequences of that change be?*

Owen, 1991, p.89

A distant place could be described as any that the pupil is not personally familiar with. Learning activities designed to help pupils answer such questions about distant places must therefore be geared towards helping the pupils develop a sense of place (or at least some familiarity with it) and identifying with the people. In order for this to happen pupils need:

- a mental map of where this place is;
- visual images of what the place looks like;
- a sense of what it feels like to live there.

The first of these requirements is probably the hardest to achieve, especially for those pupils who have little or no experience of travelling. For them, even nearby places will seem distant and unknown. Giving a sense of how far away a place is can be attempted by simulating a journey there through a story or drama. In the case of some schools and classes there may be pupils who have visited or lived in distant places like Bangladesh; their experiences can be shared. Describing the time taken to travel to a distant place can also help, as can plotting flight paths or using a globe.

The second requirement is, in theory, easier to achieve, as it can be done through photographs and film. There is a danger, however, of giving biased images. For example, in the case of Bangladesh, TV news clips probably concentrate on flooding disasters and people in trouble. Nevertheless, pupils can increase their awareness of bias if they are helped to look at images critically. This can be achieved by asking pupils questions such as:

- Who took this film or photograph?
- What were they trying to show?
- What didn't they show?
- What message were they trying to give?

For the third requirement to be achieved authenticity is very important. How else can pupils get a sense of what it feels like to live somewhere else unless it is from the people themselves or someone who has been there? Videos, tapes, letters or transcriptions of interviews with local people are ideal, though some of the sense can be lost in translation (if this is necessary). Again, it is important that pupils are helped to look critically at such information, since the people who are giving their views may not be representative.

The strategies suggested above should enable pupils to develop a sense of place about anywhere that is not familiar to them. At the same time their locational knowledge can be developed in a meaningful way. In this way pupils will also be developing knowledge about different places and how they are changing.

> *Not a superficial capes and bays type of knowledge, but an insider's knowledge, a sixth sense, an understanding of what makes a place unique.*
>
> Owen, op. cit.

This quotation reinforces the idea that teaching about places need not mean a return to the didactic and content-heavy teaching and learning associated with the 'areal' tradition that was described in the introductory chapter.

For an example of how a sense of place can be developed see Figure 10 which summarises one of the lessons from the flooding in Bangladesh unit of work. This lesson attempts to answer some of the questions posed at the beginning of this section (p.46). It mainly addresses the statements of attainment from AT2 as shown below. Notice the opportunities for differentiation of pupils between statements 3d, 4e and 5c. The final statement given (6c) relates to the national rather than local scale and would be one that the more able pupils might work towards.

Statements of attainment (AT2) relating to study of a village in Bangladesh

Level   Statement of attainment

3d   compare features and occupations of the local area with the other localities specified in the programme of study.

(4b   describe how the landscape of a locality outside the local area has been changed by human actions.)

4e   describe how the daily life of a locality in an economically developing country is affected by its landscape, weather and wealth.

5c   explain how the occupations, land use and settlement patterns of a locality outside the UK are related to environment and location.

6c   explain the variety of geographical conditions in an economically developing country specified in the programme of study, and the influence of these conditions on the distribution of population.

Assessment and evaluation

Assessment includes ways of determining what a pupil, knows, understands and can do. Evaluation includes the measurement of success of the teaching and learning programme. In Chapter 5 it was suggested that assessment and evaluation should be built into the planning of a teaching and learning programme rather than tacked on at the end of a teacher's plans.

Purposes of assessment

The most commonly cited reasons teachers give for assessing pupils include to:

- determine what pupils know, understand and can do;
- identify and build on pupil strengths;
- identify any difficulties pupils are having with their learning in order to set goals for the future;
- provide a record of pupil progress for the pupils themselves, the teacher and others (e.g. parents);
- encourage and motivate pupils;
- provide the teacher with feedback about the effectiveness of teaching strategies.

TATs can meet any of these purposes as can the assessment which teachers carry out when, for example, marking work, questioning pupils or observing pupils at work.

Assessment methods

Figure 12 provides a list of the variety of assessment methods used by teachers. This is not an exhaustive list. It is important to provide a variety of methods in order to maximise opportunities for pupils to achieve positively. This is because most pupils will be more confident in performing certain types of tasks.

Method of assessment	Example
Lesson observation	Teacher records individual pupil achievement during a practical activity, e.g. using a compass, clinometer, or weather equipment.
	Teacher records oral answers pupils give to their questions possibly using a set of criteria.
Extended writing	Pupils write a letter representing a viewpoint on a controversial issue.
	Pupils write an essay or respond to an open-ended question in writing.
'Open book' test (pupils can refer to their own work or other resources)	Pupils write a review of what they have learnt at the end of a sequence of lessons.
	Pupils answer structured questions relating to what they have recently learnt.
Objective test	Pupils answer: - true/false questions; - multiple choice questions.　Pupils complete: - a sequencing task; - a pair matching task.
Structured questions	Pupils use a stimulus or data to answer a series of questions.
	Pupils use a stimulus or data to make a decision about an issue using a sequence of questions.
Enquiry	Pupils undertake an ongoing piece of work in which they investigate an issue by collecting, describing and analysing data and making decisions.
Self-assessment	Pupils check their work against a set of criteria.
	Pupils write an evaluation of their contribution to a group.
Oral assessment	Teacher records the individual contribution of a pupil to group work.
	Pupils make an oral presentation to the teacher.

Figure 12: *Different methods and examples of assessment*

Involving pupils in the assessment process helps pupils to become aware of their own strengths and weaknesses and so to take more control of target setting. Thus they are more likely to be motivated. This can be done by:

- negotiation, e.g. the teacher and pupil discuss evidence of achievement together;

- asking the pupils to assess themselves using criteria;

- simply asking the pupils to say how well they think they did.

An example of the latter is given in Figure 13. This form was used to assess skills performed whilst on a fieldcourse.

FIELDCOURSE ASSESSMENT

| Name _____ |
| Geography teacher _____ |
| Tutor group _____ |

Pupil comments should include the following:

1 Highs and lows of the day with reasons;

2 The contribution you made to whole group and small group work;

3 How well you think you did the fieldwork and used the necessary skills.

Teacher comments should include use of skills, attitude and contribution to the day's work.

Activity/skills	Pupil comments	Teacher comments
TRAIL ■ observation ■ fieldsketching ■ direction ■ transect construction		
FOREST USES ■ listening ■ recording information ■ observation ■ sketching		
FARMING IN THE NATIONAL PARK ■ listening ■ discussing ■ interviewing ■ evaluation ■ comparison		
TRAIL ■ using a map ■ creativity ■ recording ■ group work ■ observation		

Figure 13: *An example self-assessment sheet used to involve pupils in the assessment process whilst on a fieldcourse*

Teachers can use whatever assessment method they deem appropriate when measuring achievement against statements of attainment. However, individual statements of attainment seem to lend themselves to different methods (as shown in Figure 14). In some cases statements of attainment appear to include more than one part. Take for example AT3 5c (see Figure 14). This statement requires knowledge and understanding about:

1   the causes of river flooding;

2   the effects of flooding;

3   different methods used to reduce the flood risk.

Statement of attainment	Some suitable assessment methods
AT1 4d: measure and record weather using direct observation and simple equipment	Teacher observation or enquiry
AT3 4c: identify parts of a river system including sources, channel, tributary and mouth	Objective tests or lesson observation (teacher asks the pupil questions)
AT3 5c: explain the causes and effects of river floods, and methods used to reduce flood risk	'Open book' test (end of unit review), extended writing, or enquiry
AT3 6c: explain the main components and links in the hydrological cycle	Objective test (matching or sequencing) or structured questions
AT5 6b: explain how conflicting demands can arise in areas of great scenic attraction	Lesson observation (teacher records individual contribution to a group planning exercise using criteria)
AT5 4b: discuss whether some types of environment need special protection	Oral assessment (pupil presents the case for and against protection of a particular environment and gives decision) Extended writing (report for the Minister for the Environment presenting the cases for and against protection of certain areas)
AT4 8C: analyse the causes of uneven economic development in and between countries and make an appraisal of actions and policies intended to redress such imbalance	Oral assessment (pupils make a radio documentary at the end of a unit of work) Extend writing (report or essay)

Figure 14: *How statements of attainment lend themselves to methods of assessment*

For this type of statement to be assessed pupils need to complete the relevant teaching and learning programme. A summary or review task, probably as extended writing, would be most appropriate as an assessment method here. In other cases statements lend themselves more readily to assessment whilst the pupils are experiencing the learning. For example, AT1 4d or AT5 6b can be assessed as pupils are 'doing' or discussing.

For this reason, designing the TAT to fit the purpose would seem to be essential. It is also important to avoid bias in the way TATs are presented to pupils and the conditions in which they are set. Many pupils do not perform well under pressure. Therefore TATs are an ideal opportunity to make assessment more 'pupil friendly' and simply a normal part of learning.

A further issue when planning TATs relates to whether teachers differentiate between pupils of differing abilities by task or by outcome. In the mixed-ability lesson example (Figure 10), differentiation had to be by task since pupils working to the higher levels needed different content. Many teachers would agree that, wherever possible, differentiation should be by outcome. This gives pupils the opportunity to achieve any of the levels rather than being limited. This can be implemented when statements of attainment relating to a particular topic progress through a series of levels, as shown in the second example lesson in Figure 8.

In addition to the National Curriculum assessment objectives there may be times when teachers wish to assess other learning. This might include concepts or skills from the cross-curricular themes, a wider range of skills, or value and attitude development. There is a lot of scope for assessment of objectives from other National Curriculum subjects too. One example is given in Figure 15. This is a checklist derived from the NCC English Consultation Report (AT1: Speaking and listening) which could be used to assess individual contributions to groupwork.

Collecting evidence and making judgements about attainment

Teachers need to collect and make a record of key examples of when they judge a pupil to have achieved a statement of attainment. SEAC point out that evidence gained through discussion, observation and questioning should be taken into account when judgements are made and recorded (1991). These records can be built up in a number of ways:

- collecting and filing pieces of pupil work (e.g. writing, annotated maps, tape cassettes);

- keeping checklists of criteria on which to record achievement of individual pupils;

- writing comments in a notebook whenever a pupil demonstrates attainment informally (e.g. during class discussion, question-and-answer sessions or as the teacher is observing or questioning individual pupils).

In the case of the last method it is suggested that teachers keep a notebook for each class. Within the notebook a couple of pages could be kept for each pupil on which any evidence of achievement is noted as it is observed.

These records and items of pupil work can then be used to moderate judgements with colleagues. Only through discussion about 'how and why particular judgements have been made [will teachers develop] consistent interpretations of statements of attainment' (SEAC, op. cit.) and what a pupil needs to do to achieve them. Whenever possible, pupils should be involved in the process of deciding when a statement has been achieved and selecting pieces of work for the records. This will again help with motivation and give pupils a clear idea of their progress.

Skill \ Level	3	4	5	6	7	8	9	10
LISTENING	Fair span of concentration in listening to other pupils	Takes part as a listener	Listens in order to respond constructively	Listens in order to understand the contribution of others	Listens in order to interpret the statements of others	Listens in order to convey complex information	Listens critically	Listens critically with concentration
DISCUSSING	Asks and responds to questions	Comments constructively on what is being discussed	Contributes and responds constructively to discussion, including developing ideas. Advocates and justifies a point of view	Contributes considered opinions/clear statements of personal feelings to discussion	Interprets other contributions, plays an active role in discussion and contributes constructively to the development of an argument	Takes an active part, contributing constructively to the sustained development of the argument. Interprets alternative points of view with accuracy and discrimination	Takes an active part, displaying sensitivity and being self-critical; responds to the ideas of others	Takes a variety of leading roles, e.g. taking the chair, noting down salient points
COMMUNICATING IDEAS	Some comments made	Comments made	Constructive comments made and understood	Clear statements of ideas made and considered opinions	Expresses a point of view clearly and cogently	Expresses points of view on complex matters clearly and cogently	Expresses a personal point of view on a complex subject persuasively, cogently and clearly	Expresses a point of view on complex subjects, persuasively, cogently and clearly
GROUP PRESENTATION		Takes part in the presentation	Plans and participates in a group presentation	Plans, organises and participates with fluency				

Figure 15: *Assessing individual contributions to groupwork: an example checklist for teachers to use during observations*

It may also be helpful to have a summary chart of the statement codes for each pupil. This can be kept as an ongoing record of which statements have been achieved.

To summarise, it is important to:

1   collect key examples of pupil achievement;

2   discuss judgements with colleagues;

3   involve pupils and keep them informed;

4   keep an ongoing record of which statements a pupil has achieved.

Wind energy: An example of teaching and assessing activities

This section relates to the unit of work on wind energy described in the last chapter (see pp.34–5). Reflections will be made on some learning activities which were used for assessment purposes.

An early learning activity in the wind energy unit involved a practical piece of work in which pupils recorded wind speeds and temperature around the school. Each pupil worked in a group of three and had access to equipment including an anemometer. On their return to the classroom, pupils produced a choropleth map to show the data. They were then asked to describe the results in terms of prevailing winds and turbulence around buildings. Pupils produced a remarkable consensus of opinion in their individual maps of the school and were able to articulate an understanding of why some places were hotter or windier than others.

Assessing a practical piece of work really requires observation of the pupils at work. However, due to the constraints of time it was not possible to observe every pupil making direct observations. With hindsight, a recording sheet on which to note the success or otherwise of each pupil in relation to AT1 4d or 6e would have been helpful.

Example extracts from pupils' final reports are reproduced in Figure 16a and b. Both pupils are of below average ability in their year group. Both had made direct observations of some aspects of the weather using simple equipment, and recorded their measurements in map form. Therefore, they both seem to have satisfied AT1 4d ('measure and record weather using direct observation and simple equipment'). AT1 6e is not easy to interpret ('measure and record weather using scientific instruments and procedures'). They had used scientific instruments (compass and anemometer) though it is debatable whether they had used scientific procedures and their method of data recording was unsystematic. On the whole it would seem that none of the pupils attained this higher level. Allowing for more able pupils to do so could be built into future instructions given to pupils.

The second lesson to be described was really the culmination of the topic. The pupils were asked to produce a 'flier' for the public about the proposed Dovey Valley wind farm. It was hoped that this would enable pupils to synthesise all the information collected in relation to the proposal. The activity touched on seven SoAs, covering a range from level 4 to 7, some of which had been visited earlier in the scheme (see Figure 8).

Measuring the Wind Speed.

In friday's lesson Mr Owen took a group of us out side to
measure the wind speed in different parts of the school.
The equipment we used was an anemometer and a tube was
used to measure the wind speed in kilometers per hour. We
measured the wind on the field and between the gym and
the sports hall, and by Mr. Bunford Jones' room.The
maximum speed was 50 and the least was 25 kmph.

by Andrew walsh 2B.

(a)

Windspeeds Around The School

 We split up into groups and went around the
school to measure the diffrent windspeeds.
We recorded the results and put them on a
map of the school grounds. We coloured
different parts in different colours
depending on the windspeeds.

By David Denham 2D.

(b)

Figure 16a and b: *Extracts from the final reports of two pupils on their investigations of weather around the school campus*

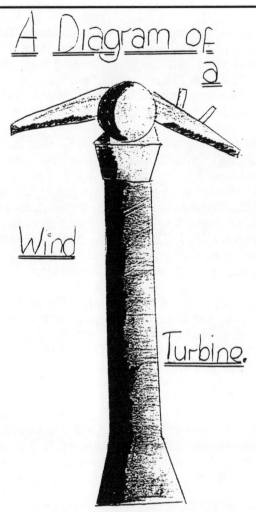

A Diagram of a

Wind

Turbine.

What are the other benifits of having wind farms not power stations.

wind turbines are a clean source of electricity. They do not produce any pollution and are safe to run. There are no risks of inflation of the fuel costs as the wind is free.

wind turbines in windfarms do not consume large amounts of land although windfarms stand over large areas over all, the machines are widley spaced with in them.

which do you want?

I know!

(a)

THE CHOICE IS YOURS!

Would you prefer to use electricity generated by coal fired power stations, which spew out into the atmosphere a noxious cocktail of sulphur and carbon dioxides, or even worse a nuclear power station which poses a great threat to everyone and churns out tons of radioactive gunge. OR, a wind farm which is totally pollution free except maybe for a slight visual intrusion on the Mid Wales landscape. As it is now there are only 9 wind turbines in Britain, where as it would only take around 4000 sq. km. of land to build enough wind turbine to generate 20% of the electricity used in the country. The price of this electricity is the same if not cheaper than any other way of producing energy. The size of one of these turbines is less than a coal-fired power station's cooling tower and only slightly taller than one of the 45,000 electricity pylons in the country (which we are all used to). All this and no radioactive pollution, no addition to the green house effect, totally renewable and explosion free. The site we have chosen in Mid Wales is an ideal spot to erect a windfarm

THE CHOICE IS YOURS!

SUPPORT OUR CAMPAIGN.

(b)

Figure 17a and b: *Examples of pupils' work*

Figure 17a and b shows two examples of the outcomes of this task. These pieces of work represent a gradation of attainment. Piece a is largely descriptive and contains text which appears to have been selected and copied from various sources. Piece b is the more successful in synthesising information from different sources. The factual content is clearly presented and the pupils' position is argued coherently and persuasively.

So how do these pieces of work match up to SoAs? The most obvious problem is that although seven statements are touched upon, only one or two are explicitly addressed in each piece of work. For example, whilst all the pupils were concerned with a proposed change in a locality (AT2 4c) and its effect on Wales (AT2 6a), none of the pupils dealt with this directly. It is therefore difficult to show evidence that either of these statements have been achieved. The problem is with the style of writing. The statement requires pupils to 'give an account of' (AT2 4c), whereas this task requires them to write for a specific audience.

However, these pieces of work do demonstrate differing levels of ability in the 'matching of styles to audience and purpose' as required in the English Order (see English AT3). Creative writing such as this may well prove to be valuable evidence of a pupil's progression and attainment in English and should not go unnoticed.

In order to maximise the pupils' opportunity to achieve SoAs, they need a much tighter brief. For instance, they could be told to include an account of the proposal (AT2 4c), describing how it will effect the local area (AT2 6a). They might also be told to make clear from their account what is meant by terms such as 'renewable' and 'non-renewable' (AT5 5b). This reinforces the need to fit assessment tasks to their purpose.

General observations about assessment of this unit

1   Several statements are visited more than once in a unit. This allows useful reinforcement of ideas and is helpful before assessment takes place. It also allows pupils who are absent to catch up on ideas they have missed.

2   Some lessons only touched on one statement. It is tempting to regard these as wasted opportunities. However, these lessons proved to be enjoyable and valuable experiences for the pupils.

3   Overall, there were more opportunities to 'visit' level 4 statements than any other but there was sufficient extension to stretch the more able pupils who were working towards level 7.

From the experience of piloting some National Curriculum assessment, it is clear that assessment must be built into the planning of any unit and individual lessons. Thought must be given to ways of setting tasks in order to give maximum opportunity for pupils to attain statements.

Evaluating the effectiveness of teaching and learning

It has been suggested that assessment procedures and evaluation criteria, set at the course outline and unit planning stages, can be used to evaluate the success of any teaching and learning. By doing this teachers find they can identify ways in which the effectiveness of a teaching and learning programme can be improved.

Another method that some teachers use is to monitor what happens in the classroom while a lesson is being taught. For example, a teacher might want to find out how to explain difficult concepts, or how individual pupils contribute to group work. In order to do this colleagues observe each other or data is collected in other ways (e.g. using a video or tape cassette). This method is known as 'action research' and has been used as a form of evaluation by a number of teachers involved in GSIP. This project developed a sequence of questions for teachers to ask themselves when adopting an action research procedure, including:

1 What do I want to focus on?

2 What do I already know about this?

3 What might be worth trying out?

4 How can I try it out?

5 What happens when I try it out?

6 Why does this happen?

7 What should I do next? (e.g. report to colleagues, change teaching strategy, etc.).

(Corney, 1991)

Conclusion

This chapter has demonstrated the variety of factors a teacher needs to take into account when planning, teaching and assessing the National Curriculum for geography, including individual needs and the variety of teaching and learning strategies and assessment methods available. An important conclusion to be made is the need for teachers in a geography department to share the work load and support each other in developing, firstly, their existing classroom practice and, secondly, effective teaching and learning for the new curriculum.

Q Tasks

Teaching and learning: individual needs

1 a) Select any unit of work which you plan to teach in KS3.
   b) Take a topic or activity from that unit and consider ways of making women and different race groups more visible whilst providing positive images of them (see p. 41).
   c) Decide how you could monitor and evaluate its effectiveness.

2 Select a topic that seems to have a progression in statements of attainment and develop a mixed-ability lesson or activity that allows pupils to achieve appropriate levels by outcome. For example, try AT4 2a, 3b, 4b, 4c, 5b, 6b, 7b, 8b for urban patterns and processes.

Enquiry learning

3 Refer to Resource 4 which contains some statements about the conditions needed for enquiry learning to take place.
   a) Add any important statements that you think are missing.
   b) Rank the statements according to your level of agreement with them. This could be done as diamond ranking (i.e. fewer statements in the top and bottom ranks and more in the middle).
   c) Select any statements which you would like to develop further or do not already achieve in your existing practice (these should not be statements with which you disagree).
   d) Decide how you will achieve these in the short and longer term.

Assessment

4 Select three existing pieces of work from pupils of different abilities on a topic that features in the programme of study or use the examples in Figure 16. Remind yourselves of the objectives of the task.
   a) Individually mark the work and decide which, if any, statements of attainment have been met.
   b) As a group discuss the judgements you made about these pieces of work in relation to the original objectives.
   c) Try to reach a consensus about statements of attainment pupils have achieved if any are relevant.
   d) In the light of this suggest ways in which the task and its objectives might be developed to improve the pupils' opportunities of meeting statements of attainment appropriate to this topic.

References

Balchin, W. G. V. (1972) 'Graphicacy', *Geography*, **57**, pp. 185–95

Barnes, D. (1975) *From Communication to Curriculum*. Penguin

Beddis, R. and Dalton, T. (1974) Geography for the Young School Leaver Project. Nelson

Boardman, D. (1983) *Graphicacy and Geography Teaching*. Croom Helm

Boardman, D. and Towner, E. (1979) *Reading OS Maps: Some problems of graphicacy*. Teaching Research Unit, Department of Curriculum Studies, Faculty of Education, University of Birmingham

Bradford, M. G. and Kent, W. A. (1977) *Human Geography*. Oxford University Press

Bruner, J. S. (1966) *Towards a Theory of Instruction*. Harvard University Press

Bullock, A. (1975), *A Language for Life*. HMSO

Chorley, R. J. (1965) *Frontiers in Geography Teaching*. Methuen

Clammer, R. et al. (1991) *Geography Today* 1–3. Collins (National Curriculum edition)

Coates, B., Johnston, R. J. and Knox, P. L. (1977) *Geography and Inequality*. Oxford University Press

Corney, G. and GSIP teachers (1991) *Teaching Economic Understanding Through Geography*, Geographical Association

Corney, G. (1991) 'Economic and Industrial Understanding Through National Curriculum Geography', Geography Schools and Industry Project/Banking Information Service

DES (1986) *Geography from 5 to 16*, Curriculum Matters 7. HMSO

DES/WO (1988) *National Curriculum Task Group on Assessment and Testing – A Report. HMSO*

DES (1990) *Geography for ages 5 to 16*. HMSO (Final report of the Working Group)

DES (1991a) *Geography in the National Curriculum (England)*. HMSO

DES (1991b) *Geography in the National Curriculum: A short course for pupils at Key Stage 4*. HMSO

Fisher, S. (ed.) (1983) *Ideas in Action*. World Studies Project

Geographical Association *Teaching Geography* (see 1991–92). Geographical Association, 343 Fulwood Road, Sheffield

Gill, D. (1983) 'Anti-racist education: of what relevance in the Geography curriculum', *Contemporary Issues in Geographical Education*, **1**, pp.6–10

Hacking, E. (1991) 'Preparing for Life in a Multicultural Society', in Walford, R. (ed.) *op. cit.*

Hart, C. (ed.) (1985) *Worldwide Issues in Geography*. Collins

Herbertson, A. J. (1905) 'The Major Natural Regions: an Essay in Systematic Geography', Geographical Journal, **25**, pp. 300–309

Hickman, G., Reynolds, J. and Tolley, H. (1977) *Project Handbook Geography 14–18*. Macmillan

Huckle, J. (module co-ordinator) (1988) Global Environmental Education Programme Teacher's Handbook and 10 units. WWF and Bedford College of Higher Education with the Richmond Publishing Company

Huckle, J. (1991) 'Reasons to be Cheerful', in Walford, R. (ed.) *op. cit.*

Lambert, D. (1990) *Geography Assessment.* Cambridge University Press

Naish, M., Rawling, E. and Hart, C. (1987) *The Contribution of a Curriculum Project to 16–19 Education.* Longman

NCC (1989) *English Consultation Report,* NCC

NCC (1990a) *Curriculum Guidance 3: The Whole Curriculum.* NCC

NCC (1990b) *Curriculum Guidance 4: Education for Economic and Industrial Understanding.* NCC

NCC (1990c) *Curriculum Guidance 7: Environmental Education.* NCC

NCC (1990d) *Curriculum Guidance 8: Education for Citizenship.* NCC

NCC (1991) *Geography Non-statutory Guidance,* NCC

Owen, A. (1991) 'A new way of looking at the world' in Walford, R. (ed.) *op. cit.*

Peet, R. (ed.) (1977) *Radical Geography.* Methuen

Piaget, J. and Inhelder, B. (1969) *The Psychology of the Child.* Routledge and Kegan Paul

Pike, G. and Selby, D. (1988) *Global Teacher, Global Learner.* Hodder and Stoughton

Rampton, C. (Chair) (1981) *West Indian Children in our Schools.* HMSO

SEAC (1991) *Teacher Assessment at Key Stage 3.* HMSO

Simmons, I. G. (1974) *The Ecology of Natural Resources.* Edward Arnold

Slater, F. (1982) *Learning through Geography.* Heinemann

Stamp, D. (1930–63) *Regional Geography* courses. Longman

Stenhouse, L.A. (1970) *Humanities Curriculum Project.* Heinemann

Walford, R. (ed.) (1991) *Viewpoints on Geography Teaching.* Longman York Publishing Services

Whatmore, S. and Little, J. (undated) 'Gender and Geography', *Contemporary Issues in Geography and Education,* **3,** 1

White, G. F. (1974) *Natural Hazards: Local, National, Global.* Oxford University Press, New York

Womankind (Worldwide) (undated) *Women's Lives 2 and 6.* Womankind (Worldwide), 112 Whitechapel Street, London

Yi Fu Tuan (1974) *Topophilia.* Prentice Hall